Kathy has figured out
also lightening the lo
Faces, is filled with wi
hope, help, and a ray

may be on. The book also shows us how to reach out and help others
suffering. Kathy even offers virtual meetups to discuss the book with
groups.

> — **Pam Farrel**, author of 50+ books including bestselling *Discovering*
> *Hope in the Psalms*, co-director of Love-Wise.com

Incredibly practical and unfortunately relevant, *7 Trials Every*
Woman Faces, offers come-alongside wisdom, laughter, and plenty of
application. Who knew Job could be so fun? Seriously, you'll giggle,
grimace, and then shift to gratitude that you can work through this
current batch of trials with a good friend.

> — **Jane Rubietta**, international speaker and author of zillions
> of words, including *Brilliance: Finding Light in Dark Places*

In *7 Trials Every Woman Faces*, Kathy Carlton Willis helps us
understand how to grin our way through life's ups and downs. If you're
ready to tackle your troubles with insights gained from humorous
to heartbreaking true-life stories, this is your book. You'll love the
straight-forward life strategies.

> — **Marnie Swedberg**, international leadership mentor
> & conference speaker, www.Marnie.com

This book is that companion you need to walk you through the trials
of your present season. Kathy uses honest storytelling, humor, and
solid theology to guide all of us on our Job-like journeys to a posture
of hope.

> — **Dorina Lazo Gilmore-Young**, author, speaker, contributor
> for DaySpring's (in)courage, Widow Mama Collective

It is fitting that this book is branded *The Grin Gal's Guide to Trials*,
because Kathy truly serves as a gentle and wise guide through the
journey of suffering. She leads us closer to Christ with a beautiful mix
of personal stories and a wealth of questions. No matter the wound
or worry, her reflections on the book of Job and fresh insights speak
healing to those tender places. This book is Kathy's life opened up to
us, her heart on the page. What a gift!

> — **Jana Daigle**, writer, rare disease patient and advocate
> LBSW, pastoral care at Praise Church

Kathy addresses the *7 Trials Every Woman Faces*, but this is no basic book. She shows that it's the *way* we deal with hardship that helps us cope and determines the outcome. Chapter one offers a fundamental tool to help my clients recognize their struggles with self-doubt by examining Job's life and responses. As a mom of six, I find the *Family Chat* and *Family Legacy* sections particularly helpful.

> **– Jenny Broaddus**, MS. Ed., LPC, psychotherapist, mom of six

Kathy has navigated more than her share of trials. She keeps humor on speed dial as she guides readers through the practical and biblical resources in *7 Trials Every Woman Faces*. Two sections, *Points to Ponder* and *Instruction for Living* direct the reader to look both inward and upward. Her focus on moving forward is most valuable in this stellar book.

> **– Deb DeArmond**, author of *Bumper Sticker Be-Attitudes, Related by Chance, Family by Choice*, and more

With Kathy's uplifting stories and insightful Bible teaching, I believe *7 Trials Every Woman Faces* will become the go-to book for thriving in the midst of trials. Kathy walks readers by the hand through their struggles and gives them a new perspective. As a relational wellness life coach, I especially like the section on difficult conversations. When you face uncomfortable situations head on, you really *can* grin again!

> **– Linda Goldfarb**, author of the *LINKED Quick Guide to Personalities* series board certified Christian life coach

How can someone who has endured such an extraordinary number of trials be known as the Grin Gal? You'll learn that and a whole lot more from author Kathy Carlton Willis. In her honest, lighthearted writing style, Kathy layers experiential and biblical wisdom with humor, hope, and solid advice. Wondering if Job is a member of your family tree? This book is sure to be a big help!

> **– Twila Belk**, the Gotta Tell Somebody Gal, speaker and author of *The Power to Be: Be Still, Be Grateful, Be Strong, Be Courageous*

I personally have dealt with all *7 Trials Every Woman Faces*, and also see them in my *Chronic Hope* ministry. We seek *anything* to lessen the roar of pain. I appreciate Kathy's biblical and practical method of dealing with suffering, while also adding a hint of humor to kindle our spirits. While overcoming many trials, God's light shines through her recalibrated smile. My whole heart endorses this book!

> **– Monique Gillming**, founder of Chronic Hope, complex regional pain syndrome fighter

7 Trials Every Woman Faces shows how to find God's perspective and in Kathy's endearing way, offers tools to overcome. The leader's guide helps facilitators create a warm circle for girlfriends to laugh together, console one another, and handle life's trials. I highly recommend this book for the Jesus girl who desires to overcome, rather than *be* overcome by life's most difficult places.

> — **Nan Jones**, speaker, Bible study teacher,
> author of *The Perils of a Pastor's Wife*

The engaging, relatable way that Kathy tackles our Job-like challenges in *7 Trials Every Woman Faces* left me feeling understood, ministered to, and better-equipped to respond to situations in a Christlike way. As The Relationship Advocate, I love the family-album format of the chapters—each including grin-inducing anecdotes, thought-provoking questions, and specific solutions.

> — **Shel Harrington**, family law attorney, speaker and blogger
> at www.shelharrington.com, The Relationship Advocate

Kathy examines Job's trials to illustrate God's faithfulness through crises. With suggestions from Scripture plus reflective questions, Kathy leads us into deeper insight. *7 Trials Every Woman Faces* will be a welcome companion to whatever life difficulties the reader is going through. Grab a Bible, pen, tissue, chocolate, and friends and prepare to see trouble in a new light.

> — **Gail Goolsby**, speaker, life coach, author of *Unveiled Truth:*
> *Lessons I Learned Leading the International School of Kabul*

No one likes to suffer and struggle. How we choose to handle our trials determines the conclusion of the painful chapters in our life stories. Kathy's in-depth examination of Job's suffering in *7 Trials Every Woman Faces* gives us both insight and hope. She helps us cope biblically and learn how to comfort others going through similar struggles.

> — **Dawn Wilson**, founder of Heart Choices Today, columnist
> at Crosswalk.com, www.upgradewithdawn.com

This year I read the book of Job, and for the first time ever, I related to him. Kathy's *7 Trials Every Woman Faces* reminded me why—because suffering is universal. Kathy's life experience and solid knowledge of biblical truth offers readers hope for whatever they're going through, as well as tools to support others.

> — **Jeanette Hanscome**, www.jeanettehanscome.com, author
> of *Suddenly Single Mom: 52 Messages of Hope, Grace, and Promise*

As a hospice nurse, I deal with many who struggle through trials. Part of my passion is providing helpful resources. I heartily recommend *7 Trials Every Woman Faces*. Kathy brings a special blend of humor and vulnerability as she supports readers with biblical insights and practical action steps.

> — **Helen Bauer**, RN BSN, CHPN, hospice educator and consultant co-host of *The Heart of Hospice* podcast, www.theheartofhospice.com

As I read through Kathy's book, *7 Trials Every Woman Faces,* I wondered how it was possible for The Grin Gal to continue to find her grin. The answer is through her faith. Keep this book within reach and allow it to activate clarity and healing. Kathy authentically shares hard stories of hurt, but also hope of healing through Christ.

> — **Kolleen Lucariello**, author of *#beYOU: Change Your Identity One Letter at a Time,* co-executive director of Activ8Her, Inc.

It's impossible to choose a chapter in this useful guide that provides the most wit, wisdom and value! Each chapter's topic contains a biblically-sound process to glean the most out of life's trials . . . with a grin! Kathy's book has the answers and steps you need to make the most out of life's trials.

> — **Mary Aucoin Kaarto**, author of *HELP for the LAID OFF, HOPE for the LAID OFF,* and *PRAYERS for the LAID OFF*

One of the chapters in *7 Trials Every Woman Faces* shows how to handle disappointment when we encounter unmet and unrealistic expectations. Kathy somehow makes facing these challenges easier with her practical takeaways, humor, and warmth. It helps to know you are not alone.

> — **Leigh Powers**, writer and speaker, *Renewed: A 40-Day Devotional for Healing from Church Hurt and for Loving Well in Ministry*

If you want to learn how to overcome Job-like struggles, *7 Trials Every Woman Faces* is for you. I like how Kathy hasn't allowed her personal pain to be wasted and she helps us see how God can redeem our suffering.

> — **Lori Moody**, Southern Baptist of Texas women's ministry representative, Double Honor Ministries facilitator

The Grin Gal's Guide to Trials

7 TRIALS EVERY WOMAN FACES

Is *Job* a Member of My *Family Tree?*

Kathy Carlton Willis

3G BOOKS

7 Trials Every Woman Faces
©2020 by Kathy Carlton Willis
www.kathycarltonwillis.com

ISBN-13: 978-1-7330728-2-3

Published by 3G Books, Beaumont, TX 77706
www.threegbooks.com

Unless otherwise noted, Scripture quotations are taken from the Holy Bible, New Living Translation, copyright © 1996, 2004, 2015 by Tyndale House Foundation. Used by permission of Tyndale House Publishers, Inc., Carol Stream, Illinois 60188. All rights reserved.

Scripture quotations marked ESV are from The Holy Bible, English Standard Version. ESV® Text Edition: 2016. Copyright © 2001 by Crossway Bibles, a publishing ministry of Good News Publishers.

Scripture quotations marked MSG are taken from *THE MESSAGE*, copyright © 1993, 2002, 2018 by Eugene H. Peterson. Used by permission of NavPress. All rights reserved. Represented by Tyndale House Publishers, Inc.

Scriptures marked NKJV are taken from the New King James Version®. Copyright © 1982 by Thomas Nelson. Used by permission. All rights reserved.

Scripture quotations marked NIV are taken from THE HOLY BIBLE, NEW INTERNATIONAL VERSION®, NIV® Copyright © 1973, 1978, 1984, 2011 by Biblica, Inc.® Used by permission. All rights reserved worldwide.

Scripture quotations taken from the Amplified® Bible (AMPC), Copyright © 1954, 1958, 1962, 1964, 1965, 1987 by The Lockman Foundation. Used by permission. www.Lockman.org

Edited by Stephenie Hovland

Interior and Cover Design by Michelle Rayburn
www.missionandmedia.com

TABLE OF CONTENTS

INTRODUCTION

E ver wish you had a friend who really understood your situation? If you had just *one* friend like that, you'd feel enough support to make it through, right? Let this book be your friend for the next little bit. It's like I'm coming alongside you, as if we have gone through common circumstances.

Believe it or not, all life trials can be narrowed down to the same categories as the afflictions Job experienced. This Bible-based *Grin Gal's Guide* is inspired by one of my personal coping skills. I've faced quite a few challenges and tragedies and witnessed them in others close to me.

Whenever I feel like I have a "kick me" sign on my back, I jokingly ask, "Is Job a member of my family tree?" Somehow this coping skill helps to laugh a little and to recognize that I'm never going to go through a trial that others haven't faced. We all go through the same stuff in life, but how we deal with the struggles determines our perspective and our outcome. We'll cover seven trials every woman faces. Just remember, no pain is wasted—it qualifies us to be a support system for others. Hopefully it equips us to be compassionate cheerleaders, unlike the miserable commiserators Job found in his friends.

Everyone a*wfulizes* their own life experiences and feels like their trials are so unique that no one can possibly relate or understand.

That leads to thinking we deserve to be pitied and are allowed to be depressed. It's sort of tongue-in-cheek to compare our lives to Job's life, but it refers to the proverb that there's nothing new under the sun—the same trials we endure, others have suffered before us.

I often pray for my husband Russ's patients in hospice (he is a chaplain). One day Aunt Billi heard my prayer this way, "We pray for Russ's patience, as he ministers." She asked for clarification, gobsmacked because the Bible says the way we develop patience is to go through trials. She warned that we don't want to ask for more trials and suggested we might not want to pray for Russ to have patience. We had a big laugh when I explained I was praying for his *patients*. When I retold this story to Russ, he said, "So *that's* what happened. A prayer miscommunication!"

> We all go through the same stuff in life, but how we deal with the struggles determines our perspective and our outcome.

You're not reading a dry memoir, although it is saturated with rich, real-life stories. You will relate to the common issues I address in each chapter and see Job's trials with personal perspective. It's common for us to cry out to God when:

- Family fails our expectations.
- Friends betray us.
- Church community rejects us.
- Health crumbles.
- Medical professionals make mistakes.
- Finances plummet.
- Others question our faith.

Whenever I rehearse my struggles, I end it by saying, "But God . . ." That helps me keep it in the proper perspective, so I don't develop distorted thinking. God laughs at the word *impossible* and sees every trial as a way to be mighty in our weakness. He says, "Kathy, I'm possible." Our enemy likes to bury us in self-pity. This book will help you live in the midst of your trials with a healthy mindset that mirrors the attitude of Christ.

I've learned not to allow difficult circumstances to define me as a victim or martyr. One way I lighten my load is to find the humor in a situation. I've laughed. A lot. It's possible. I've heard it said that laughing and crying release similar chemicals in the brain, and both are very therapeutic. During these struggles, God dries my tears and increases my joy. Grinning and laughing can be acts of worship—acknowledging his goodness in the midst of difficult circumstances. Do you think Job discovered a similar balm to his own trials?

The takeaway message is that everyone has trials; it's how we handle each trial that determines not only the end results but how we cope when we're in the midst of it. If you feel like you're waiting for the other shoe to fall and the next challenge to surface—this book will come to the rescue. You aren't alone.

> God laughs at the word *impossible* and sees every trial as a way to be mighty in our weakness.

Why Did God Bother?

I wonder why God even bothered talking to Satan about noticing Job. Or for that matter, why did he talk to Satan at all? It boggles my mind that he would waste his breath. But for whatever reason (his ways are not our ways), God talked to Satan. In the opening of Job we see God bragging about his servant Job—commenting on how righteous he was. Satan disagreed and challenged God. Then God permitted Satan to test Job's faithfulness. It's interesting to see that Satan had to ask God's permission to test Job. Is that always the case? If so, when Satan messes with me, does he first obtain God's consent?

It seems to me the Bible sets up the premise that no one before or after Job was ever tested as intensely as Job was tested. His trials included:

- Loss of health
- Loss of ten children
- Loss of wealth
- Marital stress
- Loss of community status

Satan reasoned that Job's faithfulness was only because God protected Job from any trials that would give him opportunity to curse God. This protection is described as putting a wall or hedge of protection around Job. Satan was certain Job would curse God if he lost all he held dear. God gave Satan permission to challenge Job and see just how faithful Job was to God. We know the end of Job's story, but we're still living our own personal stories without knowing how they end. The way we choose to deal with each trial determines how we write the end of our stories.

> It's how we handle each trial that determines not only the end results but how we cope when we're in the midst of it.

While Writing This Guide

History has a way of repeating itself—and so do trials. I originally studied Scripture in 2011 to go along with my question "Is Job a member of my family tree?" Then I presented it as a study to an online group. In 2015 I revamped the material and led it with a church Bible study group. While getting ready to launch *The Grin Gal's Guide to Joy*, my book team asked what the next guide would be so they could start praying for the project. I hadn't really thought about it, but evidently my subconscious had, because I said in hushed tones, "The Grin Gal's Guide to Trials." Everyone in the room said at once, "Yes . . . that's what we need."

What a contrast, to go from joy to trials, but truly, the two go together. I warned my team that I'd need them to ramp up prayers for me, because whenever I write on the topic, it appears in neon lights in my life. It's not like I didn't already have enough experience in the seven trials every woman faces. My life story already qualified me to be an expert on the subject.

But that isn't all. That request for prayer was on January 10, 2020. I sensed more trials were coming. On January 16, just days before the launch of *The Grin Gal's Guide to Joy*, my husband was laid off from work. The hospice patient numbers dropped, so they had to let several people go.

For the next month or two, we had major adjustments and prayers regarding joblessness and unemployment. Russ applied for positions and had promising interviews but no job offers.

Then on Friday, March 13, the COVID-19 pandemic put our country in lockdown. No one was hiring then. In addition to that, due to my chronic medical issues, I was deemed high risk and self-isolation was vital to my health. If that wasn't enough, I had twenty-one speaking programs cancelled. That was my main way to spread the word about *Guide to Joy*. So a book I had just birthed was languishing in sales due to lack of opportunity.

> The way we choose to deal with each trial determines how we write the end of our stories.

All was not lost! Russ was one of the few hired to new employment during the lockdown, and he began serving as a hospice chaplain again. I pivoted with some of my speaking programs and made them available online. I didn't sell books that way, but at least I was able to help others, which is the main purpose of the books.

And I revamped this book. Even though I started writing it in 2011, the time wasn't right. Then when I revisited it again in 2015, it wasn't ready. But now . . . now I've lived these themes enough for this book to be ripe for release.

Some other trials that happened during the decade of writing this book are included throughout the chapters ahead:

- I almost died of sepsis and respiratory failure during a long-term hospital stay that resulted in subsequent home health care once discharged.

- I struggled with complications from thyroid cancer, surgery, and treatment.

- Shoulder surgery and physical therapy failed, leaving me impaired until God performed a miracle.

- We endured the pain of being rejected by our church family, which meant picking up the pieces to start over.

- I had additional surgeries, post-surgical infections, and another long-term hospital stay.

- I moved to a new location with no friends or family except my spouse.

- Hurricane Harvey, Tropical Storm Imelda, and Hurricane Laura hit in my back yard—literally.

- And so much more.

The hard part about trials is that it feels like life is going on without me. Everyone else is moving forward, and I'm stuck in timeout. Just that feeling alone makes me feel misunderstood, neglected, invisible.

Here's an example from the pandemic. While others are allowed to resume being at church onsite, I'm still having to worship at home due to being high risk. Isolation feels so—well—so isolating! Trials are like that. They separate us from our support system if we let them.

All the things that made me feel rooted as I was celebrating the launch of *The Grin Gal's Guide to Joy* are gone now, except for love.

The stability of my spouse's job disappeared during those difficult months. I missed the community of our church small group, which didn't survive the pandemic and was disbanded. I no longer felt anchored to my town and church. And I'm asking if that will change, like it changed for Job (he lost much, but he gained much). I'm already looking for what God is going to add in to my life to redeem what was lost. It appears another move might be in my future, to transplant us closer to Russ's new employment. As this book goes through editing, my beloved forever home has been listed on the market for sale.

> **Trials are like that. They separate us from our support system if we let them.**

Yes, this book is for you. But evidently, it's for me too. Let's dig in together as we evaluate the *7 Trials Every Woman Faces.*

Chapter Sections

Each chapter is divided into the following sections, to go along with the *Family Tree* theme:

- **Family Album**

  This section includes word snapshots of real-life stories—some serious, some humorous—all heartwarming. Not all are from my own life—but they come from my observations on life, whether I experienced it, witnessed it, or someone else shared it with me.

- **Family Bible**

  It's important to discuss how to overcome the trials we experience from a biblical perspective. I'm calling this section *Family Bible,* because I'm reminded how families have a family Bible they pass down from generation to generation. It records births, deaths, and often contains a pressed flower. But it also possesses the underlined Scriptures deemed important or inspirational by our ancestors.

- **Family Recipes**
  Families also pass along recipes from one generation to another. If we could pass anything on to our descendants, it would be the life recipes that will help them grow and experience success God's way. This section includes life application suggestions, or action steps, with discussion questions for personal discovery. Self-help books fail if they focus only on self, so this section provides practical steps from God's guidance to help you create a better life trial verdict.

- **Family Legacy**
  Living out our faith with other people is the final stage of the process. We leave a legacy by what we invest in others. Ministering, serving, supporting, encouraging—these are the actions and attitudes that will outlive us long after we're gone. We'll learn how to best help others struggling to deal with their own trials.

- **Family Chat**
  This section contains final thoughts on each of the seven trials. It discusses some of the takeaways our focus group had when we went through the book together. Imagine your family calling for a family meeting—that's what this is. When you see these names mentioned, you'll know they were part of that focus group: Robin Steinweg, Deanna Smith, Hally Wells, Vickie Price Taylor, Kim Whaley, Sandra Reid Bassett, Robin Grunder, and Luanne Lopez.

Here's a sneak peek into each chapter:

When I'm Doubted

You can't go through life many years without someone doubting you. Others made wrong assumptions about Job, too. Naysayers questioned him. They didn't offer the benefit of the doubt, which I like to call *the benefit of grace*. What can we learn from Job and other Bible passages that will help us when our own conflicts surface? How can we overcome feeling hurt and avoid growing bitter? How will this experience help us prevent future misunderstandings from occurring?

When I'm Disrespected

Job's so-called friends judged and condemned him for sins he never committed. How can Scripture help us as we endure false allegations and grown-up bullying? Is there something we can learn to prevent it? How can we reach out to our enemies and reach out to other victims too?

When I'm Deserted

Job must have felt alone. He lost all his family except his wife, and she wanted him to curse God and die. His friends let him down. A religious leader was no help. If you've ever felt invisible or abandoned, this chapter is for you. Sadly, we don't outgrow cliquish behavior—most adults face a time when they don't feel accepted. What does God want us to learn from these times, and how can we help others, so they don't feel alone when they endure isolation?

When I'm Deceived

Job received advice from five individuals. As accurate as their words sounded, they weren't appropriate for the setting. Today, more and more believers are attacked by spiritual abuse from ministers, church leaders, or other false teachers. In this chapter you'll be encouraged to discern truth and learn to reject spiritual advice that is twisted or distorted. And you'll receive soothing comfort as you seek to heal from the spiritual bullies of your past, so you can help others who are going through the same nightmare.

When I'm Disappointed

While there's not much mention of it in Job, we can see that he was frustrated by his remaining relationships after his children all died on the same day. It's safe to say he dealt with unmet and unrealistic expectations with his wife and friends. In this chapter we'll address the hurts that hit closest to home—those inflicted on us by, or because of, the ones we love most. We'll deal with these disappointments, learn to adjust our expectations of others, and help them adjust their expectations of us.

When I'm Disabled

Not only did Job lose his relationships, he lost his health. He suffered excruciating symptoms, and when he needed the comfort of others the most, they ostracized him. Anyone who deals with acute or chronic health conditions can relate. Learn new coping skills as you suffer, and allow yourself to grieve the loss of your health. Then, with a healthy perspective, reach out to others who are enduring similar afflictions.

When I'm Destitute

What words of comfort and strength can you find from Scripture to help you hold on to hope?

Satan wiped out all of Job's possessions and material goods. He had to start from scratch. If you've ever lost a job, a home, or had a financial reversal, you know the challenge of starting over. What words of comfort and strength can you find from Scripture to help you hold on to hope? This chapter will help you when you feel destitute and equip you to encourage others as they face similar challenges.

Family Hope Chest

At the end of the book there is a section called *Family Hope Chest* that includes resources to help you deal with trials.

Added Features

Leader Discussion Guide: The back of the book includes discussion questions that can be used in small groups or Bible studies.

Grin Gal Pal: Consider finding a Grin Gal Pal while reading this book. Encourage and pray for your pal. See each other as accountability partners for any of the action steps you decide to take in *Guide to Trials*. The more transparent you are during your Grin Gal time, the more support you'll receive as you face up to the trials going on in your everyday lives.

Bible Version: All Bible verses not otherwise noted are taken from the New Living Translation.

It Starts Now!

Don't forget our main Scripture concept as we study the types of trials Job faced. *No test or temptation that comes your way is beyond the course of what others have had to face. All you need to remember is that God will never let you down; he'll never let you be pushed past your limit; he'll always be there to help you come through it* (1 Corinthians 10:13 MSG).

Closing Prayer

Heavenly Father, help me receive the support I need to cope and hope. As I read through the first chapter, reveal the truths you want me to see, and encourage my heart. Help me not get distracted or discouraged as I read. It's hard when I feel like I'm going it alone. Thank you for providing the peace and comfort I need to overcome what is overwhelming me. May I find someone else to encourage, as you equip me through this book and your Word. Amen.

Note: First names with asterisks in the book indicate names that were changed to protect individuals from any negative reflection. The story is important, but shaming someone is not the intention.

Chapter One

WHEN I'M DOUBTED

Y ou can't go through life many years without someone doubt-ing you. Others made wrong assumptions about Job, too. Naysayers questioned him. They didn't offer the benefit of the doubt, which I like to call *the benefit of grace*. What can we learn from Job and other Bible passages that will help us when our own conflicts surface? How can we overcome feeling hurt and avoid growing bitter? How will this experience help us prevent future misunderstandings from occurring?

If you've ever been misunder-stood or questioned, this chapter is for you. If others have assumed the wrong thing about you or jumped to negative conclusions, you will relate to our frustrating topic. It's a common life prob-lem. You'll figure out the best

> I'm so glad I can pray to God without having to worry about my words being misunderstood.

ways to avoid this dilemma and to remedy it if you are on either end of the conflict. First, let's open the family album and take a look at some miscommunication stories.

Family Album

What I Meant Was . . .

"To add just the right amount of style in my foyer, I'm looking for an interesting umbrella stand," I told my friend Vickie.

She said she had one I could borrow for my open house, in case I didn't find one in time. I went to her home to pick up the desired stylish container. Instead, with eyes beaming, Vickie proudly thrust this big, gawky wrought iron base into my hands. "Here you go!" she said, glad to be of help.

"Uh, Vickie? This is not what I had in mind at all. I said an umbrella stand."

"Do you need the umbrella to go with it? I've got a big striped green one I'm not using, and it would look great on your deck," Vicki said.

It was then that the aha! lightbulb clicked on in each of our minds. We both understood *umbrella stand* to mean different things.

Not wanting to hurt her feelings, I could have hid my disappointment and just thanked her for her offering. Then I would have dragged the umbrella stand home and left it in the garage until the open house was over. But, believing honesty is the best policy, I explained what I really meant, and we had a good laugh over the matter.

I wonder how many times I think I'm making perfect sense, and others interpret my words to mean something else? Words are powerful, but they have limitations. Choosing words carefully, and giving our listeners just enough information for them to understand, is essential. Too much information causes overload, and too little causes questions or misunderstandings.

I'm so glad I can pray to God without having to worry about my words being misunderstood. Not only does he understand my prayers, he knows the thoughts and intents behind the prayers. He knows my heart! And, when I don't know what to say, I am reassured by knowing the Holy Spirit prays our groanings to the Father (Romans 8:26). What a gift!

How are words treating you lately?

Kids Say . . .

Children come up with some pretty amazing notions. One time, a young girl from the church my husband pastored kept asking her grandmother when they would get to go to church. She was relentless. Exasperated, the grandmother asked the little girl why she was so eager for it to be church time. The innocent youth then asked, "Well, won't the Savior be there?"

To which the grandmother replied, "Why, yes, the Savior is everywhere. Besides, the Bible says where two or three are gathered in his name, he is there."

The granddaughter's persistence continued. She grew impatient. With hand on hip, she asked her grandmother, more clearly this time, "Mee Maw, are you *sure* Savior Willis will be at church today?" She had confused the word *Pastor* with the word *Savior.* It was a delicious moment, and my husband just ate it up!

> When we talk to God, I wonder if he is as amused by us as we are of silly children?

We all have stories of children saying the craziest things. It makes you speculate where they come up with some of their thoughts and ideas. Either their imaginations get the best of them, or they confuse grown-up talk and try to interpret it through their immature minds.

When we talk to God, I wonder if he is as amused by us as we are of silly children? Perhaps the prayers we pray contain morsels of foolishness created from the fact that our immature minds cannot comprehend the grown-up nature pertaining to the concepts of God. There is no way we can talk on the same level as God. The Bible says our thoughts are not God's thoughts (Isaiah 55:8–9).

But still, God desires that special time with us, his children. Just as our days are brightened by time spent with young people, God is pleased to spend time with us. He longs for us to slow down enough to share even more of our lives with him. The song "In The Garden" describes it this way:

"And he walks with me, and he talks with me, and he tells me I am his own; and the joy we share as we tarry there, none other has ever known."

I've been known to tell others I'm going on an Andy walk. ("And he walks with me . . . ") They assume Andy is going with me. Now you know what I really mean! God enjoys time with us, even if we spend half of it trying to figure out life through our imperfect lenses. Let's spend more time listening than talking, so we can develop a more mature perspective.

Lady Killer!

My nephew (I'll call him Mr. T) was born and raised in Japan. At the age of five, Mr. T came to the States for a visit, and we could already tell he'd grow up to be quite attractive. He has that perfect combination of inner charm and outward comeliness. I mentioned to him that he was going to be a lady killer when he grew up. You probably can anticipate the outcome of the conversation. I learned it's best not to use clichés when talking to someone who speaks English as a second language. Mr. T looked indignant and said, "I no kill ladies!" It took a while to explain the meaning.

We all have communication glitches like that. We think we are making perfect sense, but the other party hears something completely different. No wonder we deal so often with being misunderstood or perceived incorrectly. Our words get in the way.

Family Bible

Question of the day: which is more supportive, for a friend to sit by you in silence or to offer you their perspective on why you are suffering? What if their advice is based on distorted perceptions? What if you didn't ask for advice—in fact you didn't ask for them to come? Job endured friends like this.

In the course of a day he received a series of messages notifying him that he lost almost all he held dear—his livestock, his servants, and his ten children. Job's initial reaction was to mourn. He shaved his head and dressed in sackcloth and ashes. Even in his grief he continued to praise the Lord.

Trying to turn up the heat on Job's afflictions, Satan negotiated for permission to be able to torment Job, and that's when the horrible skin sores started (probably something like leprosy). As Job attempted to make sense of it all, the ones closest to him were no help. We'll talk more about his relationships in another chapter. For now, let's focus on how Job's friends misunderstood and doubted him. When Eliphaz, Bildad and Zophar came to comfort Job, they did not even recognize him—the physical afflictions were so severe. They participated in the same rituals of mourning, tore their clothing, and sat in silence with Job for seven days. Bible experts believe they remained silent for a week out of respect for Job's grief—another Jewish tradition.

> On the seventh day, Job spoke. That's all it takes to be misunderstood.

On the seventh day, Job spoke. That's all it takes to be misunderstood.

These friends gave advice based on an inaccurate assessment of Job's life. They assumed he didn't have enough faith. That he had unrepented sin in his life. Eliphaz told Job God was mad at him because of his sin (Job 5). "Rinse and repeat" again, this time with Bildad, who told Job that his misfortunes were his own fault. He said Job continued to suffer because he hadn't repented of his sin (Job 8). Zophar told Job he was being punished for—you guessed it—unconfessed sin so severe it deserved serious suffering (Job 11).

Job's friends didn't understand, so they assumed the wrong things. Their premise was that a loving God wouldn't allow suffering without cause. Isn't that the same false teaching we hear today when religious leaders claim believers will see their trials disappear if they have enough faith?

Job didn't set out to be misunderstood. We don't either. But sometimes our pure motives get buried and we're stuck—not advancing as we hoped.

Getting Unstuck

When dune buggy drivers learn to speed across the desert sand, they must figure out the right touch on the gas and clutch pedals in order to skim the surface rather than sink. If by chance they spin out too much, the wheels get buried in the soft sand. The only way out of the rut is to put it in reverse and go backward for a bit and then try again with a different approach.

> Assumptions almost always disappoint and confuse.

Often the more we mean something for good, the more it is misunderstood. We get buried and stuck despite the best intentions. Others can't read our minds, and what they do is read between the lines—the wrong way. Assumptions almost always disappoint and confuse. And when we try to explain, we often make things worse—going deeper rather than getting out of the mess. The only way out is to back up. But even then, we can't undo the damage that's already been done.

Sometimes we have to not try so hard to get the other person to understand. We have to leave the misunderstanding alone and move on, hoping truth will eventually shine a light of insight on the situation and come to our defense. Other times it's appropriate to try to clear the air.

Hidden insecurities can cloud a person's ability to understand. In the Old Testament, Saul misunderstood David's attempt to honor him. He didn't trust David, because in his mind David was the enemy—the competition. Saul wasn't a balanced individual, and that unhealthy perspective caused him to grow angry, spiteful, and bitter. After David killed Goliath, we see a taste of this poison.

> *When the victorious Israelite army was returning home after David had killed the Philistine, women from all the towns of Israel came out to meet King Saul. They sang and danced for joy with tambourines and cymbals. This was their song: "Saul has killed his thousands, and David his ten thousands!"*
>
> *This made Saul very angry. "What's this?" he said. "They credit David with ten thousands and me with only thousands. Next they'll be making him their king!" So from that time on Saul kept a jealous eye on David.* (1 Samuel 18: 6–9)

Saul misunderstood David. David served out of loyalty and obedience, for the greater good of his nation. But Saul grew jealous. That jealousy started out because of Saul's own insecurities.

The family tree of misunderstanding looks like this:

- The other party starts out feeling insecure.
- You do or say something with good intentions.
- The other party grows jealous.
- The other party wants you to fail or be harmed in some way to make himself look better.
- Words are often said to perpetuate that goal.
- Misunderstandings happen.

Even though Saul assumed David was after him, David declared multiple times that he would never harm the Lord's anointed. So the opposite happened. Saul pursued David and intended to do him harm—to stop him in his tracks. We can see from Psalm 59, three biblical responses based on David's insights for when we're misunderstood.

1. **Depend solely on God.** *You are my strength; I wait for you to rescue me, for you, O God, are my fortress* (Psalm 59:9). David acknowledged the source of his strength (God). He knew the right course of action when being misunderstood; wait for God to rescue him. And he recognized God as a place of security during his time of need. Do we pray for God to deliver us when bad things happen rather than taking matters into our own hands? Pain inflicted on us by others can cause us to seek God or seek revenge.

2. **Pray for the one hurting us.** David did not do this. Instead he prayed, *Destroy them in your anger! Wipe them out completely! Then the whole world will know that God reigns in Israel* (Psalm 59:13). This is one of those times when we need to see the contrast between Old Testament and New Testament conflict resolution. David lived in the days of the Abrahamic covenant that allowed for Genesis 12:3 (NKJV), *I will bless those who bless you, And I will curse him who curses you.* But we are in the age of grace.

   Let's see what the New Testament says our action is to be. *"You have heard the law that says, 'Love your neighbor' and hate your enemy. But I say, love your enemies! Pray for those who persecute you!"* (Matthew 5:43–44). Romans 12:14 explains it further, *Bless those who persecute you. Don't curse them; pray that God will bless them.* This is one of the hardest concepts to grasp. There are times God avenges our pain and deals with our enemies. There are times, because we've offered grace, that they turn to the Lord.

3. **Rejoice in the Lord.** *But as for me, I will sing about your power. Each morning I will sing with joy about your unfailing love. For you have been my refuge, a place of safety when I am in distress* (Psalm 59:16). When we recognize God's power and love, we have a safe and secure place in the middle of our stressful situation. Refuge means not only our shelter of protection, but also our sanctuary—our most cherished, sacred place.

We can provide an opportunity for the light of truth to clear up the misunderstanding if we are willing to walk in that truth. Jesus told Nicodemus, *"But whoever does what is true comes to the light, so that it may be clearly seen that his works have been carried out in God"* (John 3:21 ESV). We risk not clearing up misunderstandings when we aren't willing to be transparent and authentic in our actions and attitudes.

> When we recognize God's power and love, we have a safe and secure place in the middle of our stressful situation.

Sometimes, God leads us to not resolve the misunderstanding. I think of Jesus being falsely accused before the crucifixion. He could have revealed truth and defended himself. But he knew in the bigger plan for the greater good, he needed to stay silent. Occasionally, that's what God calls us to do. He is our advocate, and we don't need to be defensive. This can especially be a good spiritual exercise when it's a matter of denying self. (Learning to worry less about what others will think of us.) Let Jesus be our example. *He did not retaliate when he was insulted, nor threaten revenge when he suffered. He left his case in the hands of God, who always judges fairly* (1 Peter 2:23).

Family Recipes

Ingredients to Resolving Misunderstandings

1. Make sure each side has all the details necessary to understand a situation without assuming the wrong thing. If you don't

have enough information, ask questions before jumping to conclusions. *Don't jump to conclusions—there may be a perfectly good explanation for what you just saw* (Proverbs 25:8 MSG).

2. Ask if you can clarify the situation when someone misunderstands you. *Short-tempered people do foolish things, and schemers are hated* (Proverbs 14:17).

3. Use *I*-focused statements rather than *you*-focused statements to prevent the other party from feeling defensive. If you start a sentence with "you," it is perceived as an attack. If you start with "I," the focus is more on how you are feeling and how you are affected by their behavior. By doing this, you take ownership of your reactions, and there's less blame attached. Example, "I feel frustrated when you come late for our lunch appointment, because we have less time before I have to get back to work." If they feel attacked, they will get defensive and you'll never resolve the conflict. *Spouting off before listening to the facts is both shameful and foolish* (Proverbs 18:13).

> If you don't have enough information, ask questions before jumping to conclusions.

4. Don't expect the other person to read your mind. Communicate clearly and directly. One reason we have so many misunderstandings is because we think "If they love me, they should know this without me telling them." It is better to bring up a matter than to expect them to automatically know it. *Instead, we will speak the truth in love, growing in every way more and more like Christ, who is the head of his body, the church* (Ephesians 4:15).

5. When you hear gossip, train your mind to think, "I don't have enough information to discern the truth of this situation" rather than making a judgment call. Be careful with words,

especially with emotions attached. *Understand this, my dear brothers and sisters: You must all be quick to listen, slow to speak, and slow to get angry* (James 1:19). *The one who has knowledge uses words with restraint, and whoever has understanding is even-tempered* (Proverbs 17:27 NIV). Do not assume you know what the other party is thinking or feeling.

> **Intimacy with others is more important than winning in a disagreement.**

6. Go directly to the source of misunderstanding to discuss the matter. Unfortunately, some offended people try to silently absorb the offense, which is the perfect storm for bitterness and resentment. God gives a remedy so that we don't spiral into destructive behaviors and attitudes. *If a fellow believer hurts you, go and tell him—work it out between the two of you. If he listens, you've made a friend. If he won't listen, take one or two others along so that the presence of witnesses will keep things honest, and try again. If he still won't listen, tell the church. If he won't listen to the church, you'll have to start over from scratch, confront him with the need for repentance, and offer again God's forgiving love* (Matthew 18:15–17 MSG).

7. Be transparent and honest in order to restore the relationship. Intimacy with others is more important than winning in a disagreement. Get to the place where you'd rather show others you love them than show them you were right or hear them say they were wrong. *So then, let us aim for harmony in the church and try to build each other up* (Romans 14:19).

8. Control anger. Avoid saying something you'll regret. *Some people make cutting remarks, but the words of the wise bring healing* (Proverbs 12:18). *A gentle response defuses anger, but a sharp tongue kindles a temper-fire* (Proverbs 15:1 MSG). *Watch your tongue and keep your mouth shut, and you will stay out of trouble* (Proverbs 21:23). On the opposite side of the spectrum, also

avoid clamming up. *And "don't sin by letting anger control you." Don't let the sun go down while you are still angry, for anger gives a foothold to the devil* (Ephesians 4:26–27).

To Ponder

- Is it my pride motivating me to defend a matter when I'm misunderstood?

- Am I trying to control how others think of me?

- Am I driven to make sure they like me, or that I please them?

- What happens when I can't let the misunderstanding go?

When Jesus was misunderstood, how did he respond? Did he try to clear up the confusion or did he let it go without making a big deal of it? Often, when Jesus clarified a truth, it was when he knew the disciple needed the knowledge right away for the next step of growth. Perhaps when he didn't respond to a misunderstanding, it was because he knew the other party wasn't ready for a growth step. Maybe the confused individual needed to figure it out for himself. Other times he didn't illuminate a matter, because it would be a wasted effort—like casting pearls before swine.

Instructions for Living

1. Pray for the individual who misunderstood you—not just for the situation, but the person.

2. Act in kindness and grace to the one who treats you wrong.

3. Seek what is God's best for the one who judges you.

4. Don't attack the one attacking you. Don't return slander for slander.

5. Don't take credit or draw attention to being the more mature person in the matter. Go about showing Christ's love to the individual without any motive of being noticed—hoping

Jesus alone will be in the spotlight. He is the only one who can affect change on such an individual.

6. Ask God to show you what you can learn from the situation, whether or not the misunderstanding is ever cleared up.

Questions

- Can you think of a time when you felt misunderstood? How did it make you feel? How did you handle it?

- What are some ways you can communicate to others when they misunderstand you?

- Have you ever assumed the wrong thing about someone going through a tough time? Describe the situation and the outcome.

- Are you a fixer? Do you tend to offer advice rather than offering true support?

Family Legacy

Ways to Avoid Being One of Job's Friends

Let's look at Romans 12 for ways we can be better friends.

1. **Focus on the good and don't fixate on the bad.** *Don't just pretend to love others. Really love them. Hate what is wrong. Hold tightly to what is good* (Romans 12:9).

2. **Show love to others by giving them special treatment.** *Love each other with genuine affection, and take delight in honoring each other* (Romans 12:10).

3. **Don't slack off in being a true friend to God and his children.** *Never be lazy, but work hard and serve the LORD enthusiastically* (Romans 12:11).

4. **Be upbeat as you anticipate good things ahead. Wait for them to happen, and in the meantime, spend time in prayer**

over the matter. *Rejoice in our confident hope. Be patient in trouble, and keep on praying* (Romans 12:12).

5. **Show your love by having a welcoming spirit and a giving heart.** *When God's people are in need, be ready to help them. Always be eager to practice hospitality* (Romans 12:13).

6. **If others mistreat you, continue to bless them, and do not give in to the temptation of revenge.** *Bless those who persecute you. Don't curse them; pray that God will bless them* (Romans 12:14).

7. **To support your friend in the appropriate manner, make sure your mood matches your friend's mood.** *Be happy with those who are happy, and weep with those who weep* (Romans 12:15).

8. **Don't be so impressed with your own knowledge that you act like you're above them. Instead, play well with others no matter their status in life.** *Live in harmony with each other. Don't be too proud to enjoy the company of ordinary people. And don't think you know it all!* (Romans 12:16).

9. **Rather than getting even with a person who has mistreated you, consider what would most honor God.** *Never pay back evil with more evil. Do things in such a way that everyone can see you are honorable* (Romans 12:17).

10. **Live in peace with others by avoiding harmful conflict.** *Do all that you can to live in peace with everyone* (Romans 12:18).

11. **Don't get defensive—instead realize God is your advocate.** *Dear friends, never take revenge. Leave that to the righteous anger of God. For the Scriptures say, "I will take revenge; I will pay them back," says the LORD* (Romans 12:19).

12. **Show practical acts of love to your enemies—see and meet their needs. They won't expect it!** *Instead, "If your enemies*

are hungry, feed them. If they are thirsty, give them something to drink. In doing this, you will heap burning coals of shame on their heads" (Romans 12:20).

13. **Don't let it get to you when others try to harm you in words or deeds. Instead, let it motivate you to respond with goodness.** *Don't let evil conquer you, but conquer evil by doing good* (Romans 12:21).

Family Chat

To avoid doubting and misunderstanding others and assuming the wrong thing about them, we need to stay plugged in to God and view others as God views them. Put our own agendas and motives aside. Give the benefit of the doubt. Invest in the other person by actively listening rather than jumping to conclusions.

It also helps to show we want to make things right rather than *be* right.

Deanna Smith, from the focus group, said this, "This study has made me aware that each of us have hearts and minds under the surface that are mulling over and seeking solutions to our situations. It gave me an opportunity to relate to what other gals are facing and pray for them. It stimulated a longing in my heart for every woman to overcome and be at peace. I have experienced a yearning to cheer others on to victory in this faith walk with the Lord. In the midst of it all, the Lord is always the answer."

> Live such a life that if others hear something about us, they will say, "That is out of character for them" and not believe the gossip or lie.

When others doubt us or assume the wrong things about us, we need to address the situation based on their frame of mind. If their agenda is to make us look bad (so they look better), then nothing we say will change that. If they are innocently mistaken, we can try to clear the air. Either way, we need to avoid being defensive and learn a way to move forward and not get bogged down sulking over how we've been mistreated. Often when we try to rectify the matter, we compound the situation and make it worse. I don't know about you, but I find that so exhausting! Live such a life that if others hear something about us, they will say, "That is out of character for them" and not believe the gossip or lie.

Closing Prayer

Father in heaven, I have experienced the pain of being misunderstood and doubted. Yet I also know there are times I've been guilty of these same attitudes with others. Help me grow as I seek your principles for dealing with this. I have a hope that is anchored in *you*, not in my own strengths or abilities. May I put down my human tendencies, pick up your godliness, and put on your lovingkindness, so I can adopt your attitudes and actions.

And Father—I'm exhausted in my obedience rather than energized in my efforts to please you and deal with all this life stuff. Help me make sure I'm acting in your strength, so I don't run out of steam on the journey. Amen.

Chapter Two

WHEN I'M DISRESPECTED

Job's so-called friends judged and condemned him for sins he never committed. How can Scripture help us as we endure false allegations and grown-up bullying? Is there something we can learn to prevent it? How can we reach out to our enemies and reach out to other victims too?

Family Album

I've had my fair share of bullies. All right—*more* than my fair share! I'm not a fan of these aggressive types who seemingly enjoy harassing and intimidating someone they perceive to be an easy target. They torment and oppress others to make themselves somehow seem more impressive—stronger.

Bullied and Sullied

Third grade came with new challenges for me. The school was just barely close enough to have to walk to school rather than take the bus. Scary thought for my mother, who still wanted to hold my hand when I crossed the street! We tried several walk-to-school rituals to give Mom peace of mind. After a while she began to trust me. I developed common sense and became safety minded. So I walked to school with my neighborhood friends and walked home with my grade-school friends.

Stella* was one of my new classmates. I wouldn't really call her a friend—more like a bully. Imagine a third-grade girl already wearing heavy-duty foundational undergarments, and you'll comprehend her girdled girth. Each day we'd walk home, and each day she'd beat me up. Even during the school day when I should have been concentrating on my class studies, I spent time dreading the walk home. It was a miserable experience. When other bullies realized I was a soft target, they joined in the games.

Third grade was also the year my sleepwalking increased. Any wonder? Too young to sort through my feelings while awake, I waited until sleep for my head and heart to process my bully problems. One night when Mom couldn't find me in the house after bedtime, she looked outside and found a tiny girl's footprints in the snow. She tracked the trail to the car—where I sat inside. She asked me what I was doing. "I'm ready to go to school, Mom. Can you drive me? It's snowy."

She answered me. "No, Kathy, it's not time for school yet. Let's go back in the house now. It's cold out." The next day I didn't remember the incident. I had slept through it all. That's about the time my folks decided the doctor and my teachers should be aware of what I was experiencing. I had a problem, and it all started with bullies.

Then a boy named Trenton* thought it was okay to throw punches at me. I'll never forget rolling down the rock-lined retaining wall from one of his blows. After a few sore ribs and hurt feelings, my dad volunteered to be my boxing trainer. He taught me how to make a closed fist punch. I'm not saying that's the right thing to do—just saying I learned to stand up for myself.

But along with learning to stand up for myself came a sense of independence. No one was ever going to bully me again. Or that's what I thought . . .

Sticks and Stones

A pastor's wife named Jan shared with me an excellent illustration. She suggested I take a tube of toothpaste and squeeze out all of the toothpaste. Then she asked me to try to put the toothpaste back into the tube. No matter how I stuffed and crammed and coerced the paste, it was impossible to fill the tube again. Then she said this is just like our words. They might come out of our mouths effortlessly, but trying to get them back is futile. What an illustration!

Proverbs 25:11 (ESV) says, *A word fitly spoken is like apples of gold in a setting of silver.* Then I read in the New Testament, Colossians 4:6 (ESV) *Let your speech always be gracious, seasoned with salt, so that you may know how you ought to answer each person.*

In the previous section, I shared about the physical jabs caused by bullies. But there were other attacks that hurt just as much—verbal ones. I was born with some sort of invisible target, I guess. For whatever reason, cruel kids called me names. (You would think I was Rudolph, and the others wouldn't let me play in any reindeer games!) I was called Pinocchio for my ski-slope nose. Cleopatra for the same reason. Then, they dropped the names, and just said, "Kathy nose." For example, "Does anyone know what time it is? Wait, Kathy nose." Those clever puns sting. In high school the nicknames were too embarrassing to even confess here.

Some bullies don't ever grow up. They simply grow meaner. My adult life has endured the worst kinds of abuse—initiated by so-called spiritual friends, bosses, and leaders. They used words to throw jabs at me.

The childhood saying "Sticks and stones may break my bones, but words will never hurt me" is just not true. Words hurt. Words destroy. But the right words can encourage and bless. My desire is to know my words are pleasing to God and helpful to others.

One way I can ensure my words are fitly spoken is to make sure my heart is right. Matthew 15:18 (NKJV) says, *But those things which proceed out of the mouth come from the heart.* Hebrews tells me that the Word of God is a discerner of the thoughts and intents of my heart. The Bible prepares my heart so I have no regrets when I speak.

> Words hurt. Words destroy. But the right words can encourage and bless.

I have not attained victory in this area, but I have seen progress. If my words are like a feather pillow, I want to have the assurance that when that pillow is emptied into the wind, I have no fear as to where those feathers will float and land. Much better to have that peace of mind than to imagine me scrambling to pick up the feathers before someone else picks them up. By then, the damage is done.

Want to have words that help rather than words that hurt? Start with the heart!

Family Bible

Job's friends went from speaking nothing to speaking harsh words of attack. It's difficult to judge the motive of these visitors (and the Bible says that's God's job), but if I put myself into the scene, I sense how hurt I would have been if I were Job. Especially considering these were the first words after a week of silence, coming from the lips of so-called friends.

What would have encouraged me? A friend praying aloud. Reaching out and touching me (even if my skin might have been contagious) while touching heaven with words of petition on my behalf. That would have ministered to me. But these men who sat with Job made statements in a way to sound like the spiritual experts of the day. Yet we know they were not mentioned as any sort of faith authority in the discussion God had with Satan when mentioning Job as a shining example. So it's possible if they sat perched on a spiritual pedestal, it was one of their own making—not one they earned or deserved.

After Job broke the one-week silence with his comments, Eliphaz replied first (Job 4). In Job 4:2 he said, *"Will you be patient and let me say a word?"* It reminds me of a time I taught a small group at a professional conference. The schedule gave us limited time. An attendee took up more than her time talking during the session. So as a good facilitator does, I carefully hooked the conversation back to segue to the next order of business. I explained we wanted to give each conferee their fair share of our time. But this gal could not be hushed.

With animated arms, she yelled at me, "Would you just let me finish!" Wow. Talk about a way to not win friends and influence people! No surprise, she didn't receive a favorable evaluation from me. Well, Eliphaz hadn't started to speak yet, but he broke in to Job's discussion and said he couldn't stay silent any longer. One way to bully others is to raise your voice, wave your arms, and take control of the conversation.

Eliphaz continued by making a list of suppositions and accusations, all starting with the word *you*. Just as if he were pointing the finger at Job. Repeatedly. In the prior chapter we learned to start sentences with *I* rather than *you* if we want to prevent the other party from feeling defensive or attacked. Eliphaz didn't know that—or didn't care.

Then in Job 4:8 Eliphaz made sure Job knew he was an expert on this subject. It states, *My experience shows that those who plant trouble and cultivate evil will harvest the same.* Aggressors love to spotlight their superior traits.

Eliphaz went on to describe a disturbing vision he had in the middle of the night (Job 4:12–21). He twisted the truth to apply it to Job, not fully knowing Job's situation. He didn't factor in God's grace and love. He inflamed the situation by pronouncing unconfessed sin in Job's life. False allegations.

Bully tactics help the accuser feel more puffed up while deflating their victims. The more Job tried to plead his innocence, the more insistent the friends became, starting with Eliphaz. Perhaps they didn't want to admit a person could suffer without it being punishment for sin, because that might mean they could be targets of the same attacks at some point in their lives. It was easier to believe Job was a sinner, and they were not.

It seems possible the three friends discussed Job's situation on their way to his place, because later on in Job 5:27, Eliphaz says, *"We have studied life and found all this to be true. Listen to my counsel, and apply it to yourself."* If Job's friends started out with good intentions when they left their homes to encourage Job, it's possible their gossip on the trip led to a change in motives. When they saw Job's horrible circumstances, they jumped to conclusions and assumed he had a sin problem. That led to them turning into self-appointed spiritual advisors.

Wonder Break

- If Job's friends were right (which they weren't), do you think they went about admonishing Job in the proper spirit?

- How should they have approached Job, if he *did* need to be aware of a shortcoming in his life?

- When you are faltering, how do you hope another will come alongside you to help pull you up out of your situation?

- When you feel moved to help a brother or sister with their spiritual defeats and flaws, how do you think it's best to approach them?

Paul gives good advice in Galatians 6:1, *Dear brothers and sisters, if another believer is overcome by some sin, you who are godly should gently and humbly help that person back onto the right path. And be careful not to fall into the same temptation yourself.*

As the rest of the story unfolds in the book of Job, we see that in the end, God vindicated Job and scolded his friends. God is Avenger and Advocate. Not only was he angry for how they treated Job, he despised how they mistreated truth. *After the LORD had finished speaking to Job, he said to Eliphaz the Temanite: "I am angry with you and your two friends, for you have not spoken accurately about me, as my servant Job has"* (Job 42:7).

Probably one of the most satisfying lines in Job, humanly speaking, is when God tells the friends, *"My servant Job will pray for you, and I will accept his prayer on your behalf. I will not treat you as you deserve, for you have not spoken accurately about me, as my servant Job has"* (Job 42:8). Did you notice how that one phrase was repeated in the course of two verses?

> When you are faltering, how do you hope another will come alongside you to help pull you up out of your situation?

Imagine if three of your co-workers mistreated you repeatedly. Then finally the boss comes to deal with the matter. He informs them only if you will vouch for them will he allow them to remain on the payroll. Satisfaction. Well, God avenged Job on much heavier matters. God didn't need Job's prayers to deal with the matter, but for whatever reason, he purposefully instructed Job to pray for these "frenemies."

How does this example from Job tie in to when Jesus said to pray for those who persecute us? I notice he doesn't merely suggest we pray for them, making it optional if we feel like it. It's a clear instruction (with no excused absences) to pray for those who hurt us.

> It's a clear instruction (with no excused absences) to pray for those who hurt us.

I once dealt with a bully boss who used intimidation tactics to try to manipulate me. When I called her bluff and resigned, she responded with an exaggerated reaction. Bullies tend to magnify matters. She took me to court. I asked our pastor (we were members of the same church) to mediate, but he refused to be involved in the matter. His lack of intervention suggested he thought the court system was better equipped to handle it. The court ordered her to pay a cash bond that she would not remit, so eventually the case was dropped. But it still cost me a full year's pay in legal fees and threatened to damage my reputation.

I felt robbed, violated, and for a while, I let the very thought of her nauseate me. But I had to learn the right way to deal with the situation, so that it wouldn't ruin me. Fortunately it wasn't my first devastation rodeo, so I knew what I had to do to clear my heart and mind and move forward, restored and renewed, ready for the next chapter of my life.

1. Experience the release of forgiveness.

> *Therefore, the Kingdom of Heaven can be compared to a king who decided to bring his accounts up to date with servants who had borrowed money from him. In the process, one of his debtors was brought in who owed him millions of dollars. He couldn't pay, so his master ordered that he be sold—along with his wife, his children, and everything he owned—to pay the debt.*

> *But the man fell down before his master and begged him, "Please, be patient with me, and I will pay it all." Then his master was*

filled with pity for him, and he released him and forgave his debt.

But when the man left the king, he went to a fellow servant who owed him a few thousand dollars. He grabbed him by the throat and demanded instant payment.

His fellow servant fell down before him and begged for a little more time. "Be patient with me, and I will pay it," he pleaded. But his creditor wouldn't wait. He had the man arrested and put in prison until the debt could be paid in full.

When some of the other servants saw this, they were very upset. They went to the king and told him everything that had happened. Then the king called in the man he had forgiven and said, "You evil servant! I forgave you that tremendous debt because you pleaded with me. Shouldn't you have mercy on your fellow servant, just as I had mercy on you?" Then the angry king sent the man to prison to be tortured until he had paid his entire debt.

That's what my heavenly Father will do to you if you refuse to forgive your brothers and sisters from your heart. (Matthew 18:23–35)

2. **Ask God to heal you and to help you get your eyes off the list of wrongs, so you can see what he has in store for your future.** *To all who mourn in Israel, he will give a crown of beauty for ashes, a joyous blessing instead of mourning, festive praise instead of despair. In their righteousness, they will be like great oaks that the LORD has planted for his own glory* (Isaiah 61:3).

3. **Pray for your wrongdoer with the same lens of unconditional love used by God. Pray for God to use whatever is necessary in their lives to bring them to a good end in him.** *"But I say to you who hear: Love your enemies, do good to those who hate you, bless those who curse you, and pray for those who spitefully use you"* (Luke 6:27–28 NKJV).

Family Recipes

Ingredients to Dealing with Disrespect

1. **Stay calm.** *"The Lord himself will fight for you. Just stay calm"* (Exodus 14:14). *Instead, I have calmed and quieted myself, like a weaned child who no longer cries for its mother's milk. Yes, like a weaned child is my soul within me* (Psalm 131:2). *A fool is quick-tempered, but a wise person stays calm when insulted* (Proverbs 12:16).

2. **Rehearse truth.** *Arrogant people smear me with lies, but in truth I obey your commandments with all my heart* (Psalm 119:69). *My eyes strain to see your rescue, to see the truth of your promise fulfilled* (Psalm 119:123). *Get the truth and never sell it; also get wisdom, discipline, and good judgment* (Proverbs 23:23). *Stand your ground, putting on the belt of truth and the body armor of God's righteousness* (Ephesians 6:14).

    Let your roots grow down into him, and let your lives be built on him. Then your faith will grow strong in the truth you were taught, and you will overflow with thankfulness (Colossians 2:7). *Through the power of the Holy Spirit who lives within us, carefully guard the precious truth that has been entrusted to you* (2 Timothy 1:14).

3. **Don't return in kind, but in kindness.** *Kind words heal and help; cutting words wound and maim* (Proverbs 15:4 MSG). *"But I say, do not resist an evil person! If someone slaps you on the right cheek, offer the other cheek also. You have heard the law that says, 'Love your neighbor' and hate your enemy. But I say, love your enemies! Pray for those who persecute you!"* (Matthew 5:39, 43–44). *"But to you who are willing to listen, I say, love your enemies! Do good to those who hate you. Bless those who curse you. Pray for those who hurt you"* (Luke 6:27–28).

4. **Guard your reputation, and live up to a good name. Others**

will respond to what is authentic and will also recognize a lie. *Choose a good reputation over great riches; being held in high esteem is better than silver or gold* (Proverbs 22:1).

5. **Pray for God to reveal truth to the spectators.** *Truthful words stand the test of time, but lies are soon exposed* (Proverbs 12:19). *"And you will know the truth, and the truth will set you free"* (John 8:32). *Therefore do not pronounce judgment before the time, before the LORD comes, who will bring to light the things now hidden in darkness and will disclose the purposes of the heart. Then each one will receive his commendation from God* (1 Corinthians 4:5 ESV).

6. **Forgive.** *Get rid of all bitterness, rage, anger, harsh words, and slander, as well as all types of evil behavior. Instead, be kind to each other, tenderhearted, forgiving one another, just as God through Christ has forgiven you* (Ephesians 4:31–32).

> Don't return in kind, but in kindness.

7. **Move on.** *Brethren, I do not count myself to have apprehended; but one thing I do, forgetting those things which are behind and reaching forward to those things which are ahead, I press toward the goal for the prize of the upward call of God in Christ Jesus* (Philippians 3:13–14 NKJV).

To Ponder

As Potential Victim:

- Do I put my trust in someone who isn't trustworthy?

- Do I believe the lies I've been told that say I'm unworthy of respect or compassion?

- Do I need to learn a new way to deal with conflict?

- Do I know how to draw healthy boundaries in my commitments and obligations as I interact with others?

- Do I have passive-aggressive tendencies as a way of asserting my own version of control in a situation or with others?

As Potential Bully:

- Do I have a judgmental attitude?
- Do others perceive that I think I'm better than them?
- Do I attack others with my words?
- Do I use manipulation tactics and guilt-trips to force others to follow my agenda?
- How can I change these bully behaviors and attitudes?
- How can I learn to have more empathy for others?

Instructions for Living

> *But Joseph said to them, "Do not fear, for am I in the place of God? As for you, you meant evil against me, but God meant it for good, to bring it about that many people should be kept alive, as they are today. So do not fear; I will provide for you and your little ones." Thus he comforted them and spoke kindly to them.* (Genesis 50:19–21 ESV)

1. How you handle adversity in life says a lot about your faith in the Lord. No one is exempt from facing trials and struggles. Life challenges can be a potential for growth or a breeding ground for bitterness, jealousy, and anger.

2. Learn to be resilient. Joseph faced a series of trials that started when his brothers sold him into slavery. He didn't stay down. Each time he was knocked down, he got back up again.

3. Don't participate in pity parties or expect others to treat you like a victim or martyr. Joseph could have easily cried out, "Life isn't fair!" Instead he looked for a new opportunity. Helen Keller said, "When one door of happiness closes, another one

opens, but often we look so long at the closed door that we do not see the one that has been opened to us."

4. Instead of wallowing in hopelessness, look for the next ray of hope. Joseph could have stayed imprisoned, not only behind bars, but in the trap of negativity. Rather than remain in bondage to the setbacks, he embraced the freedom of hope. This cleared the way for him to have good opportunities, which promoted him to the position where he could help his brothers in their time of need (and help the whole nation during the famine).

5. Adopt an attitude that even if others have evil intentions motivating their actions, God can use it for good.

6. Allow obstacles to shape your future and have a good outcome. God can help you land on your feet as you seek him.

7. There are times when someone acts despicably against you because they want to hurt you or see you in a lower place of status, thinking it will somehow elevate their own status. If you reframe the way you look at your terrible circumstance, like Joseph did regarding his brothers, it will help you cope—or even thrive despite the emotional wounds.

Questions

- **Think of the last time you caught yourself being judgmental.** What motivated your attitude? How did you handle your thoughts? How did the way you managed your attitude lead to specific actions (for the good or for the bad)?

- **What do you think happens when you address your own flaws before you start to deal with the ones for which others are guilty?** *"Judge not, that you be not judged. For with the judgment you pronounce you will be judged, and with the measure you use it will be measured to you. Why do you see the speck that is in your brother's eye, but do not notice the log that* *is in your own eye? Or how can you say to your brother, 'Let me take the speck out of your eye,' when there is the log in your own eye? You hypocrite, first take the log out of your own eye, and then you will see clearly to take the speck out of your brother's eye"* (Matthew 7:1–5 ESV).

- **What can you do when your enemies shame you?** Remind yourself that God takes care of those who oppress you. What happens to your feelings when you make it a priority to know God's ways? *To you, O LORD, I lift up my soul. O my God, in you I trust; let me not be put to shame; let not my enemies exult over me. Indeed, none who wait for you shall be put to shame; they shall be ashamed who are wantonly treacherous. Make me to know your ways, O LORD; teach me your paths. Lead me in your truth and teach me, for you are the God of my salvation; for you I wait all the day long* (Psalm 25:1–5 ESV).

Family Legacy

1. **Don't put yourself in the position of judge.** *"Judge not, and you will not be judged; condemn not, and you will not be condemned; forgive, and you will be forgiven"* (Luke 6:37 ESV).

2. **Deal with your own flaws and faults before straightening someone else out.** Be sure your vision is corrected, or the way you see the other person's situation might be blurred. (See notes regarding Matthew 7:1–5 in previous section.)

3. **Be careful what you say about others.** *Don't speak evil against each other, dear brothers and sisters. If you criticize and judge each other, then you are criticizing and judging God's law. But your job is to obey the law, not to judge whether it applies to you. God alone, who gave the law, is the Judge. He alone has the power to save or to destroy. So what right do you have to judge your neighbor?* (James 4:11–12).

4. **When you're tempted to seek revenge, instead draw closer**

to God and ask his Spirit to increase the fruit of the Spirit in your life. *Dear friends, never take revenge. Leave that to the righteous anger of God. For the Scriptures say, "I will take revenge; I will pay them back," says the Lord* (Romans 12:19).

5. **Courage comes from clinging to the strength you have in the Lord.** *"This is my command—be strong and courageous! Do not be afraid or discouraged. For the LORD your God is with you wherever you go"* (Joshua 1:9).

6. **Take refuge in the Lord.** *I love you, O LORD, my strength. The LORD is my rock and my fortress and my deliverer, my God, my rock, in whom I take refuge, my shield, and the horn of my salvation, my stronghold. I call upon the LORD, who is worthy to be praised, and I am saved from my enemies* (Psalm 18:1–3 ESV).

7. **Find a way to be content even when you are disrespected and mistreated.** *For the sake of Christ, then, I am content with weaknesses, insults, hardships, persecutions, and calamities. For when I am weak, then I am strong* (2 Corinthians 12:10 ESV).

Family Chat

It's easy to feel indignant when others don't act like I would act if I were in their shoes. Hally Wells from the focus group said, "I confess thinking, 'Well if it were *me* doing [this and that], I would *never* have done it that way. I would have responded [this way].' And because they *don't* respond like I would, I assume it's because they have a motive

> When our hearts are weak, wounded or willful, we either buck or bolt (fight-or-flight response).

to hurt me in some way." The entire group related to that and said it's helpful to remind ourselves that a different response is not always a wrong response or an intentional attack on us. How often we read the wrong thing into their intent!

43

As you're going through this book you probably know all of these steps, but feel like you're "going through the motions." That happens when I'm struggling with a "self" focus. I get stuck, or paralyzed, and it's hard to dig out. Satan loves it when that happens, because then I'm not effective for God's kingdom work.

One of the hardest things God asks us to do is to love those who hurt us. It is a great trial of our humanity! And one reason it is so difficult is because the process takes so much time.

When we have a hard time forgiving someone, it's often more about our own heart conditions than the hearts of those who did the original wrongdoing. Here's my thought on that: When our hearts are weak, wounded or willful, we either buck or bolt (fight-or-flight response).

It's always easier to clean up someone else's mess than our own. But it's only when we deal with our own struggles that we are in a position to help others.

Closing Prayer

Father, I have no words today other than "Help!" My heart grieves over the pain I see others suffering, and when I think of my own trials too. Bless all of us in a way that's unpredictable. Surprise me with your goodness in such a bold way that I can't miss it being from you. Help me cling to you when I fail everything else and have no other support. Help me get to the point where I realize you really are *enough* for what I perceive as my *lack*. Amen.

Chapter Three

WHEN I'M DESERTED

Job must have felt alone. He lost all his family except his wife, and she wanted him to curse God and die. His friends let him down. A religious leader was no help. If you've ever felt invisible or abandoned, this chapter is for you. Sadly, we don't outgrow cliquish behavior—most adults face a time when they don't feel accepted. What does God want us to learn from these times, and how can we help others so they don't feel alone when they endure isolation?

Family Album

Hand-Me-Downs

Vicki thought I was a highfalutin cousin because my mom handed down my clothes to her family. What she didn't know was that most of those same clothes were discarded from my older cousins and passed to me. For many years the only new items of clothing I had were lovingly sewn by my mom. Hand-me-downs have followed me my whole life, and I've learned the blessing of receiving someone else's castoffs.

In fifth grade, when most kids selected instruments to play in band, I wasn't afforded that option. I played clarinet, because—you guessed it—my cousin Kristy quit playing hers, and it was passed along to me. I didn't think twice about it being second-hand. Instead, I was excited for this rite of passage to join band. Sometimes castoffs lead to new opportunities.

When we were growing up, my folks had the opportunity to buy a run-down house on adjoining property. It was not fit to restore and had to be torn down. But before that happened, they pulled out some interesting antique items. In what someone else left behind, my family saw value.

> All of us want to fit in somewhere—to matter.

One of the blessings of ministry life is being on the receiving end of a lot of hand-me-downs. Not just clothing—even furniture. Probably the most interesting cast-off I ever received was a busted antique player piano! (They don't travel well, or I'd still have it.)

I've learned along the way that hand-me-downs aren't the mark of receiving charity. It's a smart way to be a good steward of possessions. Recycling at its best. Limited resources can be shared and multiplied.

More than possessions are cast off. People feel discarded—brushed off. Others they love no longer want them around. Outcast, they must find a new place to belong. All of us want to fit in somewhere—to matter. In one church that mostly ministered to the country club set, the pastor asked us to start a new ministry. It included a Sunday school class, activities, and other fellowship opportunities as a group.

Even though we didn't specify what ages or types of adults could be in our group, others like us joined the group. (It's human nature: *like* likes *like*.) Our class filled with people who didn't have any elite labels. After a month or two of gelling as a group, one of the members felt comfortable to say out loud what everyone was thinking. "Hey, we're the outcasts. You put us all together, and we no longer feel alone. There's something comforting in knowing there are a lot of others just like me!"

Several times in our lives, Russ and I have attracted others who don't feel like they belong. They don't fit in. We felt the same way, which means we found our people!

In one small group, members joined from all different demographics, and they joined the group blind—not knowing us or any others in the group. We had people from six decades of life. Married and single. Parents and childless. All different skin colors and cultures. One of the members welcomed a newcomer and said, "Our group is weird in the best possible way."

There are different terms for it: outcasts, marginalized, misfits, invisible, neglected, loners . . .

> God loves you when no one else loves you—when you don't love yourself.

If you are feeling like a castoff today, know that God loves you when no one else loves you—when you don't love yourself. He loved you before you ever came to know him. And because of his unconditional love, he will stand by you no matter what you do or say—even if you don't measure up to others or fail miserably. He adores you, and he knows you by name. You matter to him so much; nothing would do but to pay the ultimate price and bring you into an intimate relationship with him.

Don't Worry, Mommy Won't Kill You

One of my favorite clips from America's Funniest Home Videos is more of a sound bite than a visual. A young boy named Miles takes his brand-new video camera out in the snow, intending to be a very grown-up videographer. As he sleds down the hill, narrating like a sportscaster, there's a blur, and then Miles bursts into tears. His sister, the heroine in this story, comes running to help. She recognizes her job quickly, to both reassure her brother and to find that camera.

While Miles cries about how much it cost and how much they trusted him to take care of it, Sister keeps saying, "Don't worry, Miles. Mommy won't kill you." With her Southern accent, it's more like "keel" you. Then the miracle happens, and the camera is found. The clip ends with Sister saying, "Mommy won't keel you now."

There's so much I love about that clip. It could have happened to any of us—not just a small boy. Others entrust their hearts and their "stuff" to us. We want to act responsibly, but then something happens out of the blue, and before we know it, we've done the very thing we didn't want to do. We let them down. We dread the inevitable, feeling more outcast and downcast by the minute. Then our God sweeps in to rescue us, and restores us. What was lost is found.

Not all busted relationships are restored, but the holes in our hearts get patched up better than new. And just as Miles must have appreciated his sister more than ever after that loving gesture of reassurance and rescue, we learn anew every day, ways to appreciate the Savior when we feel like all is lost.

Invisi-shield?

Wonder Woman possesses this incredible stealth jet that had its own superhero feature—it could become invisible. It allowed her to show up where she needed to and disappear, taking take care of business without being caught or shot down. Quite a superpower!

Sometimes I think I have this same superpower. My vehicle definitely has invisi-shield. People pull out in front of me all the time like I'm invisible. Accidents are narrowly avoided because drivers act like they have the road all to themselves. Don't they see me?

But worse is when it seems I'm the invisible woman. I feel like waving my hand in front of the eyes of others to find out if they even see me. Instead of "Can you hear me now?" I want to ask, "Can you see me now?" There's nothing sadder than being with other people but feeling all alone. I hear everyone around me talking—to other people. Fellowship. All the relational interaction I crave. It's times like that when I wish I didn't have the superhero power of invisibility. Yet I know if I do something to get others to notice me, then my agenda is for it to be all about me. That's not good.

Self-absorption is a slippery slope. What I've learned is to find someone else who looks as isolated as I feel. I invest in them—ask questions that draw them out and make them feel special. If they project a sense of awkwardness or loneliness, I help them know they are not alone. I show them I want to know them. They matter to God, and they matter to me! Before I know it, I'm not only helping them feel a part of things—I'm no longer invisible.

> There's nothing sadder than being with other people but feeling all alone.

Alone and Hurting

We aren't novices at moving to new locations. With Russ being a pastor, we found an instant welcome in our new churches and communities. They wanted to know us and we wanted to know them. We felt connected.

When we moved to Beaumont, Texas, we knew absolutely no one. Russ transitioned into a new career as hospice chaplain. We had no church to call family, and I had no role as pastor's wife that caused people to want to know me. I was, essentially, nobody. They didn't realize I was a national writer and speaker. They didn't know why they'd want to get to know me—that I'm a great friend and a prayer supporter for those in my life. They had plenty of friends—why would they need *me*? It didn't dawn on them—I needed *them*.

Knowing church fellowship was essential to experiencing community, we tried several churches. None of them were a fit. Quickly we landed on the right church because we experienced growth and joy every time we entered the building. The worship inspired weekly revival, and the sermons challenged us and filled our notebooks with *God-wow!* moments.

Only one problem. Every week we tried to get to know people, to no avail. We tried to enter into circles of conversations. It was hard for us to put ourselves out there. Even doing all we could to get to know the staff and the congregation, it took easily a year before we started to feel connected.

What made the difference?

- Offering to serve.
- Getting involved in teams to minister to others.
- Being part of small group ministry.
- Encouraging others without trying to be in the spotlight.
- Showing up, consistently.
- Connecting on social media, so we can do life together through the week.

Once people got to know me, they said, "You were always grinning—I had no idea you were lonely."

Hurting and Alone

One of the worst times in my life was going through back-to-back surgeries in a city where I didn't know anyone. Facing a trial virtually alone reveals suppressed loneliness and allows it to intensify. My husband was at a new job, so he couldn't get off work much. Plus he had to take care of our dog and other duties in our home. I spent two weeks in the hospital with a lot of time on my hands, alone. Other than having an hour or two a day with Russ, my room was quiet.

Once a week someone from the pastoral staff came to visit. But they knew I was a former pastor's wife, so they didn't consider my spiritual needs. They checked on me, but they didn't pray over me or see if I had any other wishes or requests. None of the women from the church came to visit. My family lived too far away. It was easy for me to feel overwhelmed and unloved by the silence. It made my suffering worse, to endure it alone.

When discharged, I was left with home health visits and dilemmas of what to do next regarding the unrelenting infection and swelling. I was so overwhelmed. Who do I call? Where can I go for help? What should I do?

> Facing a trial virtually alone reveals suppressed loneliness and allows it to intensify.

All of those questions seemed much more daunting because of being alone. I didn't know where to turn for help.

God designed us for community. How did I fight back against the invitations to my own pity parties? I practiced spending time focusing on others. What needs did they have? How could I pray for them? (I certainly had plenty of time to pray!) How could I encourage their hearts?

I looked for reasons to be grateful. An apartment neighbor helped with our Boston terrier and delivered a lovely potted plant. Friends from far away sent emails. Fresh cut flowers arrived. One of Russ's coworkers brought over a meal. Even though I felt lonely, I wasn't always alone. It just seemed that way if I focused on it. So I learned to focus on the blessings.

And mostly, I didn't fight against the silence of alone time. Instead, I invited God into it with me. His presence made all the difference. I realized the saying, though trite, is true: "When God is all you have, he is all you need."

Corner Torture

Mom had me all figured out. (It's that "Mommy Psychology" that many mothers innately have!) The most effective disciplinary tactic Mom used was to put this Chatty Kathy in the 1960s version of time out—she banished me to stand in a corner, nose touching the joining walls. This worked, because it forced me to slow down, hush up, and be alone with my thoughts. No one to entertain me. No playmate. Just me and the wall and a lot of silence. I didn't like feeling alone and hated disappointing my parents.

When I had friends over, Mom would say, "Don't think you'll avoid being punished, just because you have others here—there's enough corners for everyone!" That was back in the day when there was a *mom code* that every grown-up had the discretion to discipline all offenders in order to keep the peace.

Some are more content being alone in their thoughts than others, but God didn't design any of us to be islands. We are all meant for community—for fellowship. So when we feel rejected, abandoned, forsaken—it hurts. We want to be connected emotionally and intellectually to the hearts and thoughts of others. Not fish out of water.

When we face a *life bump* that feels a lot like "corner torture," it's time to seek God as our source of connectivity. He won't leave us isolated—alone. And somehow he fills the vacancy in a way that assures us—he alone is enough—even in the corners of life.

The Corner Torture of Pandemic

As I mentioned earlier in the book, the COVID-19 pandemic really did a number on me. It put me in isolation due to my high-risk status.

In one week I went from:

- Co-chairing an IF:Gathering women's conference—to post-poning it. Now I'm co-chairing a chair.

- Hunkering down with a friend in a coffeehouse, working on our projects—to hunkering down at home working on my projects while my friends report in virtually, working on their projects at the same time.

- Serving at our church's small group ministry kiosk helping people feel connected through small groups—to helping small groups feel connected to members during this social distancing.

- Seeing lab techs being outfitted in biohazard gear to draw my blood—to getting my lab results on a video tele-med chat with my doctor remotely. I was his first virtual patient.

- Making lists for groceries and to-do lists and getting it all done—to making lists for groceries and to-do lists with not as much getting crossed off the lists! (Out of stock. Out of energy.)

- Making many plans for travels and speaking events this spring—to scratching my head and praying and wondering (not necessarily in that order).

- Marketing my book *The Grin Gal's Guide to Joy*—to sharing how it's possible to grin with joy despite COVID-19.

- Wondering when Russ would find work—to wondering how many jobs would be affected by this state of emergency.

- Claiming God's presence is enough—to experiencing anew "God's presence is enough!"

The pandemic represents a time of mourning and praise for me. Let me back up and explain. All of 2019 I prepared for 2020 by making detailed plans (plans I believed the Lord directed me to make). Most of those plans were cancelled by the pandemic.

Speaking tours. Teaching opportunities. Book sales events. Instead of being with groups of people, I am isolated and alone.

Alone in my grief. I didn't dwell long on what caused the grief but did allow myself to grieve so I could heal. By acknowledging it, I honored "what was" or "was to be." I'm reminded of how David would phrase his psalms. First he laid it all out before the Lord—everything that bothered him. But by the end of the psalm, he always praised the Lord anyhow. I've been determined to do the same—praise God anyhow!

Here are some ways I've reminded myself of God's goodness despite the loss in 2020:

- None of this took God by surprise. That is a comfort. And it helps me not regret all I lost. It wasn't *all* lost; it was just shaped differently than I originally expected.

- The isolation of pandemic inspired me to come up with new ways to encourage others and to train writers. I'm so grateful for technology that allows us to be separate but together.

- I praise God for providing a job for Russ when so many are losing theirs.

- In isolation I can reflect even more on these seven trials all women face and write from a spirit of understanding and support—true empathy.

- I am gaining perspective and wisdom because of all these things. I often grow best when I am enduring challenges and trials. God is amazing at not just recycling but upcycling what seems like garbage.

- I know that this time we are in is temporary. No matter what happens next, the very end of time is going to be amazing—heavenly even!

Not only did the grief of what was lost cause me to feel isolated, but as my area opened back up, I felt even more alone. When everyone was staying home due to the pandemic, we experienced a special survivor togetherness. But when others were allowed to go back to a new version of normal, and I had to continue to self-isolate, then I felt more alone than ever before.

> Satan knows how to magnify our perception of the situation to push us down a spiral staircase of self-pity.

In the book's introduction I mentioned asking my launch team to pray as I wrote this book. I even predicted the writing of *Guide to Trials* would cause me to experience the seven trials all women face in a whole new way. I wasn't wrong.

Family Bible

The Worm Song

There are several versions of the worm song, but the one we sing around here goes, "Nobody likes me. Everybody hates me. Might as well go in the garden and eat worms."

The fun of the song is that by the time you finish the rest of it, describing all nature of the worm kingdom, the pity party is replaced with silliness.

Yet, there's a deeper significance to the song. No one escapes the harsh reality that not everyone likes them. But even worse is when our loved ones reject us. We're not wired to cope with that sort of devastation. And often, Satan knows how to magnify our perception of the situation to push us down a spiral staircase of self-pity.

"Nobody cares. Everybody ignores me. I feel so disconnected from life. I have no friends. No one who understands me. They don't *get* me. I feel so insignificant."

Why do we rehearse such sad-sack sentiments? One of Satan's tools when we're going through a bad time is to cause us to exaggerate our sense of catastrophe. One of my friends used to try to minimize it when she called for help by saying, "I'm having a bad five minutes." Satan wants us to feel like we're having a bad *life*—with circumstances worse than what anyone else is experiencing.

It's very human to become irrational as we list our woes. We awfulize our lives. Satan tempts us to feel defeated and discouraged because he wants us to quit trying and give up.

If we pick friends who use us, then we're doomed to be hurt by them when they no longer have need for us. Some of us have a faulty friend selection device, and we end up with toxic friendships—people with whom we can't trust our hearts. Unhealthy motives come into play. If people don't have holy agendas, they may hurt those they spend time with. Other times when we feel rejected, it's our own faults because we're trying to get what we want. Our motives are skewed, not theirs.

> **We'll miss it if we spend too much time in the garden eating worms!**

When others don't treat us like we think they should, it doesn't mean we are failures. It simply means it's not God's timing. He has something else that's more important for us to learn, and we'll miss it if we spend too much time in the garden eating worms!

So how do you stop feeling alone? By connecting your heart to the heart of God. And if you've done that—is there something more you can do to grow your relationship with him? A song that has come to mean a lot to me in recent years, made popular by Barlow Girl, is "Never Alone." It acknowledges the pain of loneliness—the song's honesty is raw and refreshing. But it ends in the victory of realizing nothing can separate us from the love of God. And even though he's invisible, we can trust the unseen. We can trust our hearts to him.

Job's Wife

Job must have felt discarded by his wife when she said, "Curse God and die." But as I've considered Mrs. Job's point of view, I've come to realize that she was also under a great amount of duress and possibly didn't have the same spiritual insights as Job to help her cope with the tremendous loss. She endured all the same losses as Job except for her personal health. (Being caregiver to a loved one in a health crisis is pretty awful!)

It's possible the attitude that surfaced in her was the mindset Satan had hoped to evoke in Job—a very human response to loss. How can a person *not* take it personally when so much hits at once? Satan wanted Job to curse God. Instead, we find Mrs. Job saying those famous words "Curse God and die." She grew angry toward God when the rug was pulled out from under her, and she wanted her husband to join in her hissy fit.

How often do we get frustrated with our husbands when they don't participate with us during our tirades over what we deem "travesties" in life? Yet we jump all over Mrs. Job for being so . . . so very . . . human. It's possible she thought a quick exit from a painful life would be better than Job enduring such a long, drawn-out torture with his physical ailment, not to mention the lingering grief from their catastrophic loss.

As is typical of a person during times of serious trials, it's possible Mrs. Job couldn't see past her own suffering—she might have been self-absorbed. There are few mentions of her in the book of Job, but we see at some point she rejects Job further, turning away from him due to his bad breath, of all things. *"My breath is repulsive to my wife. I am rejected by my own family"* (Job 19:17).

I find it interesting that some commentaries claim Mrs. Job to be a tool of the devil, and others declare she is a faithful attendant to her husband's needs in his time of loss and suffering. I wonder if she had a change of heart somewhere along the way. The last time Mrs. Job is brought up in the book of Job, it's an inference rather than a direct mention. We see that she has birthed a new family with Job. She was given an opportunity to find new joy, either because of the births, or possibly before the new children even arrived.

Maybe she had to go through the stages of grief before she was ready to embrace life again. Ready to embrace her husband again, for that matter! But somewhere along the way, we see she changed. We don't know if it was a gradual adjustment or an overnight transformation, but it happened.

Until that point, though—Job must have felt abandoned, rejected, discarded. Have you ever felt that way? Discouraging times make God's servants feel more isolated and alone than they truly are.

"My days fly faster than a weaver's shuttle. They end without hope . . . I cannot keep from speaking. I must express my anguish. My bitter soul must complain." (Job 7:6, 11). When a person is depressed, they lose hope. And when a person is hopeless, they get depressed. So it's important to cling to hope!

Think of those in the Bible who were alone right before God used them in a mighty way:

- David alone in the cave.
- Jacob alone in his tent.
- Elijah alone by the brook.
- Moses alone on the backside of a mountain.
- Jesus alone in the Garden of Gethsemane.
- And our Job alone, even when surrounded by friends who don't understand.

Each experienced significant victories right after these times of feeling shut off from human interaction or compassion.

Perhaps God allowed them to be isolated from the rest of the world, so they would realize when God was all they had, God was all they needed. Maybe that's what our alone times can teach us too. We learn in the shadows what we can't learn in the pleasant sunshine. God's light dispels the darkness. We can face truths and experience the presence of God when all else is faded from view. We fear being alone, but sometimes that downtime happens right before a great big blessing.

In Job 23:1–9, amidst bitter complaints and groaning, Job discussed his search for God. He couldn't find God any-where. He hoped to find God in order to plead his case,

> **We learn in the shadows what we can't learn in the pleasant sunshine.**

knowing God would treat him fairly. In a later passage, he admitted he felt God had abandoned him—perhaps even discarded him.

> *"Oh, how I long for the good old days, when God took such very good care of me. He always held a lamp before me and I walked through the dark by its light. Oh, how I miss those golden years when God's friendship graced my home, When the Mighty One was still by my side and my children were all around me, When everything was going my way, and nothing seemed too difficult."* (Job 29:1–6 MSG)

Deeply discouraged, Job wallowed in despair and utter isolation. A common malady is to long for a time in our past when we remember life being better than this. But in this moment of despair, Job believed God was no longer taking care of him or giving him light for the journey ahead. Job 30 continues Job's discussion regarding how forsaken he felt—an outcast. Empty, alone, neglected. Job began to think God didn't notice what he was going through. In his desperation, he even wondered if God was assigning this misery to him.

In Job 31, Job took a personal spiritual inventory and concluded he was doing all God required of him, and he was indeed living a life that pleased God. In this realization he discovered something we all must learn—sometimes suffering happens whether we deserve it or not—whether we brought it upon ourselves or God allowed it for some greater purpose. But it's never for "no good reason," because God always makes sure something good can come of any pain we suffer—any tear we shed.

Even in Australia

Probably one of my favorite children's books is *Alexander and the Terrible, Horrible, No Good, Very Bad Day* by Judith Viorst. Alexander goes through a series of bad-day adventures, but he's convinced life would be better in Australia. One trial after another, he experiences a stinky day, and of course his siblings and others are having extra-good days—magnifying his misery. All day he dreams of an escape to Australia. But at the end, his mother's wisdom reassures him that everyone has a bad day now and then. It closes with a revelation that has stuck with me as one of my own go-to phrases now. "Some days are like that—even in Australia."

Forsaken

> *And about the ninth hour Jesus cried out with a loud voice, saying, "Eli, Eli, lema sabachthani?" that is, "My God, my God, why have you forsaken me?"* (Matthew 27:46 ESV)

Jesus suffered the ultimate sense of abandonment. His friends denied him in his final hours. He felt as if his heavenly Father even turned his back on him. It breaks my heart every time I imagine this event. How alone the cross must have seemed, even though there were men hanging on crosses to each side of him.

And then I remember a passage in Hebrews 4:14–16 that says: *So then, since we have a great High Priest who has entered heaven, Jesus the Son of God, let us hold firmly to what we believe. This High Priest of ours understands our weaknesses, for he faced all of the same testings we do, yet he did not sin. So let us come boldly to the throne of our gracious God. There we will receive his mercy, and we will find grace to help us when we need it most.*

Jesus understands us when we say we feel alone. He's experienced it. He lived it, yet didn't sin. Even in his suffering, he found a way for the pain to make a difference—to make the mission matter more than his feelings. What can we learn from him when it comes to feeling discouraged when we're discarded?

Family Recipes

Ingredients to Overcoming Discouragement

Count it all joy, my brothers, when you meet trials of various kinds, for you know that the testing of your faith produces steadfastness. And let steadfastness have its full effect, that you may be perfect and complete, lacking in nothing. If any of you lacks wisdom, let him ask God, who gives generously to all without reproach, and it will be given him. But let him ask in faith, with no doubting, for the one who doubts is like a wave of the sea that is driven and tossed by the wind. For that person must not suppose that he will receive anything from the Lord; he is a double-minded man, unstable in all his ways. (James 1:2–8 ESV)

1. Consider your testing an opportunity for your joy to increase. Often, when left to our own emotions, we let our discouragement increase instead of our joy.

2. When your faith is tested, you can find a dogged determination and strength you didn't know you possessed.

3. You'll mature into completeness as you allow your dedication to God be the main thing in your life.

4. Even if you don't feel like you have enough wisdom to accomplish this, you can ask God to give it to you, and he will

bestow knowledge and understanding in your mind and heart without even scolding you.

5. When you ask for wisdom, ask in faith, believing with unwavering confidence that God will accomplish in you what he wants with this opportunity.

6. Avoid waffling in your faith, because that lack of stability will keep you from experiencing the true joy that will help you overcome your discouragement.

To Ponder

- How can I use this aloneness to draw closer to God?

- Is there someone different or new with whom God wants me to connect during this time of feeling disconnected from the ones who have let me down?

- Is there anything I need to do to restore a relationship?

- Do I have my guard up or a mask* on that's keeping me from bonding with others? If so, what can I do to change that and become more open to the people God puts in my life?

- Do I have a chip on my shoulder about a strained or dysfunctional relationship? What can I do to resolve the matter?

---

*Wearing a mask has taken on a whole new meaning since experiencing the pandemic of COVID-19. We have learned that it truly does impair relationships when masks are on. The eyes say much, thankfully. But not seeing the entire face causes us to feel distant from each other and even makes it harder to hear the muffled words. Many of us have realized we read lips and need to see faces. And mostly, we've discovered how essential those grins from each other get us through the day.

Instructions for Living

> *O LORD, how long will you forget me? Forever? How long*
> *will you look the other way? How long must I struggle with*
> *anguish in my soul, with sorrow in my heart every day?*
> *How long will my enemy have the upper hand? Turn and*
> *answer me, O LORD my God! Restore the sparkle to my eyes,*
> *or I will die. Don't let my enemies gloat, saying, "We have*
> *defeated him!" Don't let them rejoice at my downfall. But I*
> *trust in your unfailing love. I will rejoice because you have*
> *rescued me. I will sing to the LORD because he is good to me.*
> (Psalm 13:1–6)

1. Talk to God about your feelings. Nothing you say will shock him or cause him to think differently of you. Better to vent your frustrations with him, so your wounds have an opportunity to heal, than to keep them bottled up or take them out on someone else. God can prepare your heart to sense his presence again in your life, when you're honest with him about what you are experiencing.

2. Once you talk with God about what you are going through, limit the time you spend thinking negatively. It only serves to defeat you and keep you bogged down from being effective for him. If necessary, designate fifteen minutes a day to rehearse the list of struggles, and the rest of the day remind yourself it isn't time yet to have that day's pity party.

3. Journal the reasons you feel abandoned by others and by God. Turn each list into a prayer, until once again you are confident that the Lord is at work in your life.

4. When you don't know what to pray, pray Scripture. Personalize it to fit your situation. God's Word is always productive and effective.

5. Learn a healthy way to deal with the antics of your enemies, so they don't mess with your head and defeat your heart.

6. The way to reverse the damage done when feeling discarded and discouraged is to trust in God's unfailing love. *Trust*— place your confidence in him. *Unfailing*—know it's up to a God who cannot fail to hold your cares for you. *Love*—he will never leave you or forsake you, even when it feels the whole world has abandoned you.

7. Rejoice in the rescue of the Lord. Know he is your rescuer even before you are completely out of trouble. All you have to do is relax and let God be your lifesaver. The more you struggle or flounder, the longer it takes to scoop you out of your hurtful circumstance. Celebrate his wondrous watchcare over you.

8. Sing aloud (and in your heart) songs of praise and thanksgiving for his goodness—not merely God's general goodness, but his specific goodness to *you*. It's virtually impossible to be discouraged while you are singing a song of praise to the Lord and truly mean it.

Questions

- **Read Psalm 22.** Verses 1–8 show David venting his frustrations and grieving his pain. But in verse 9, David's mindset changes. Then verses 12–18 recount more suffering. You probably notice the similarities in this passage and what Jesus went through on the cross. He concludes the psalm with less of a self focus and more of a Kingdom focus.

- **List five ways you relate to Psalm 22 and five ways this passage inspires you when you are feeling alone.** Do you see a prayer to pray, an action to take, or a thought to focus on?

- **What might God want you to learn about your moments of loneliness**—those times when you feel all alone in this world whether you're by yourself or in a crowd of people?

- **How can you avoid making other people feel cut off from you?** Are you guilty of brushing off people because of your busy schedule, or because you have your guard up to avoid being hurt again?

Family Legacy

1. **When you feel outcast or downcast, take refuge in the Lord.** *Be merciful to me, O God, be merciful to me, for in you my soul takes refuge; in the shadow of your wings I will take refuge, till the storms of destruction pass by* (Psalm 57:1 ESV).

2. **Knowing how much God cares for you helps you hand over your burdens to him.** *Give all your worries and cares to God, for he cares about you* (1 Peter 5:7).

> When you don't know what to pray, pray Scripture.

3. **When you feel discarded (and even when you don't), connect to the one sent to help. Don't try to handle the weight of the world on your own**. *"And I will ask the Father, and he will give you another Helper, to be with you forever"* (John 14:16 ESV).

4. **Tend to the needs of others, and know that God is tending to your needs.** When necessary, he'll send a human to take care of you. This is the mutually beneficial nature of The Golden Rule. *"Do to others whatever you would like them to do to you. This is the essence of all that is taught in the law and the prophets"* (Matthew 7:12).

5. **Practice the presence of God.** When you feel alone, meditate in an acute awareness that he is with you. *"Teach these new disciples to obey all the commands I have given you. And be sure of this: I am with you always, even to the end of the age"* (Matthew 28:20).

Family Chat

Kim Whaley from the focus group said this when thinking how hard it is that some people don't like us. "My dad shared with me something that has stayed with me for years. He said that not everyone liked Jesus, and if everyone didn't like Jesus, what makes me think I am so great that everyone will like me? Wow! That puts things in perspective." We are hardwired to want to please everyone, even though we know that is impossible. But we *can* focus on pleasing one person—our Lord.

> We can find a glimmer of hope when we know God is real and his concern for us is just as real.

Robin Steinweg mentioned when we feel all alone (or lonely even when with others), "Those times are opportunities to press in close to my Father in heaven. I can ask, 'Father, what is it you want to be for me in this?'" I like the idea of pressing in close to the Father. Draw near to him! It reminds me of the times I felt insecure—nothing would do except to be scooped into my dad's strong, very muscular arms.

Robin also mentioned that when circumstances are already awful, we are tempted to wait for even more trials to hit. We adopt a mindset that if it can get this bad, it can get even worse. She reminded our focus group that loving God and loving others is worth the risks and that "God not only has our backs—He has our hearts."

We learned from David's example in Psalm 22 that it's okay to express our distress and even dissatisfaction aloud to God. David kept it real, didn't he? Some of us have been taught to just "take our licks." If we voice our objections, it's disrespectful to God. Because of that way of thinking, many people haven't been as intimate with God as they could be. They figure if they can't say anything nice, they shouldn't say anything at all. It's okay to share all our feelings with God.

Sometimes we avoid addressing our real-life issues with God, because we don't want to sound like we're whining. We think we need to buck up. Or we are intimidated by God's *God-ness*. He designed us for fellowship—to interact with him about our everyday stuff, just like we would talk to a friend. Yes, he is high and lifted up, he is all-powerful—our everything. But he doesn't want his "God-ness" to keep us from sharing our hearts and minds with him. We don't have to feel intimidated by him. He doesn't want us to hold back any part of our lives from him.

Vickie Taylor said this about overcoming the defeat associated with trials and isolation, "Perhaps he wants me to learn not just that he's all I *need*, but to learn how to make him all I *want*."

We can find a glimmer of hope when we know God is real and his concern for us is just as real. His shoulders are big enough to bear whatever we are going through and however we feel about it at the time. It won't shock him to hear what we are thinking (he knows it anyway!). He can help us work through the situation a lot better if we tell him where we are on a matter. But if we clam up, we thwart our possibility for growth and maturity.

Closing Prayer

Father in heaven, I come to you today and ask that you take special care of me and others going through trials. Be with me as I face my burdens head-on with the new perspective you've given me. Help me acknowledge the very things I'd like to forget about in my life, whether they happened today or many years ago. Show me how to hang on when my circumstances separate me from the comfort of feeling loved by you and others. Remove the "invisi-shield" so

I can be seen—not for my own glory or pride—but so I can be a part of your effective kingdom work. Be the *balm in Gilead* that soothes my wounds and dries my tears. Help me be aware of the others feeling like outcasts around me—that I might reach out to them and show them they can belong to you. Thank you that I am never alone—even when it feels as if I am. Amen.

Chapter Four

WHEN I'M DECEIVED

Job received advice from five individuals. As accurate as their words sounded, they weren't appropriate for the setting. Today, more and more believers are attacked by spiritual abuse from ministers, church leaders, or other false teachers. In this chapter you'll be encouraged to discern truth and learn to reject spiritual advice that is twisted or distorted. And you'll receive soothing comfort as you seek to heal from the spiritual bullies of your past, so you can help others who are going through the same nightmare.

Family Album

Oklahoma Fish

Papa (Mom's daddy) loved teasing me when we visited on vacation. It was easy to pull the wool over my eyes—I was so gullible! One of his favorite pranks was when he told me we were having Oklahoma fish. It was my favorite, and no matter how many fish we pulled from the Mississippi River back home in Louisiana, Missouri, none of them ever tasted as good as Oklahoma fish. It must have been the way Granny prepared it with her special mix of

69

cornmeal. Or maybe it was the type of grease or the temperature of the gas stove. Or her specially seasoned cast iron skillet. All I knew was—it was delicious, and I ate my fill of it every time.

I'm not sure how old I was before I realized there was an extra sparkle in Papa's eyes when he asked me if I wanted Oklahoma fish for supper. Was he foolin' me? Finally the mystery was revealed. I overheard him telling another grown-up that he sure had fun messing with me over the yellow squash. Yellow squash? Aha! Finally it all fell into place for me. On the days I helped Granny cut the squash off the vines, those were the nights we had Oklahoma fish. But we had yellow squash at home—these were different. Finally I asked Granny and Papa what made the difference.

That was when I learned the power of suggestion is especially potent when introduced to a naive girl who is eager to believe. Granny sliced the squash lengthwise into fish-shaped "steaks." She prepared them like fish. So to me, they *were* fish. Only they weren't.

I used to be an easy target for deception, because I took everyone at face value. Only after years of allowing others to mislead me have I learned to not be so easily fooled. Discernment plays a big role in discovering the truth. But as a little girl, I wanted to believe my supper plate included Oklahoma fish long after I learned it was only yellow squash.

Thinking Outside the Box

During my senior year, my boyfriend Russ was a freshman at college. The first time he came home for a visit, he took me to shop for an engagement ring. He joked that he realized he looked pretty good out of the small pool of choices in our little town, but he was afraid I'd get to college and realize there were lots of fish in the sea. Truthfully, I think he missed me! We put the ring on layaway and said nothing more about it. The thought of that ring warmed my heart every time I wanted to talk to him and realized he was five hours away. I missed him too.

By Christmastime, I thought for certain he'd pull the ring out of layaway for me. Clues pointed to our pending engagement—the most obvious being a small jewelry box-shaped present under his family's Christmas tree.

Christmas morning came, and I spent a little more effort on putting myself together, just in case this was *the day*. Russ picked me up to go to his house for present-opening time. My heart started to beat faster. His sister Etta held a camera. *Was this it—the moment I'd been waiting for?* Russ put two boxes in front of me. One—the tiny box I had scoped out previously. The other—a big box. *Maybe a quilt made by Mom Willis for our hope chest?*

"Which do you want to open first?" Russ hoisted the big box closer to my feet—then pinched the tiny box between his fingers. "This one—or that one?" Almost giddy, I pointed to the itty-bitty box. *My ring! It had to be my ring!* "Very well—open it."

There was a ring box inside. *My ring!* I snapped open the case, and there inside, shining brightly for all to see—almost as bright as the flash on Etta's camera was . . . a polished rock key chain. Womp womp. *What? How could I be so wrong?* I put on a brave face and turned my attention toward the big box.

Off came the wrapping paper. The box opened to reveal—another gift-wrapped box. On and on this went, layer by layer. Until . . . until I was down to another itty-bitty box. *Could this be the one?* Then it all happened at once. I opened the case to find my ring. Etta snapped the photo. Russ hugged me and helped me put the ring on my finger. It was official—we were engaged!

Russ went to great trouble to fool me. And I took the bait—hook, line, and sinker. Or in his case—*stinker*! And I felt loved because it showed forethought. He made a plan and recruited his whole family. The extra effort (and even the prank) put a smile on my face.

But normally when someone tricks me, I just feel "the fool." I don't like it. Deception is only exciting for the perpetrator. The victim feels deflated, defeated, and disturbed.

Family Bible

Truth Detector

Were you ever spiritually deceived? Perhaps a pastor used the pulpit to mislead or manipulate you. Or church leaders pressured you through guilt trips and unhealthy comparisons. Maybe a Christian author led you away from truth by sounding *so close* to what you've read in Scripture. I've even seen spouses use the Bible and church to coerce their mates into toxic relationships. In all these cases it's a matter of power and control—abuse of power to gain control of the individual who looks up to them. Worst-case scenarios involve religious cults and domestic violence, but every day we see more common misuses of Scripture to support an unbiblical agenda.

> Deception is only exciting for the perpetrator. The victim feels deflated, defeated, and disturbed.

I have a friend who feels like she was brainwashed by her former pastor. She made unwise decisions, uncommon for her way of normal decision-making, based on the demands and directions from this pastor. When she woke up from her state of spiritual confusion and chaos, she said it felt almost like she'd had a spiritual lobotomy—like someone had scrambled her brain matter, causing common sense to disappear, to suit his whims.

This leader encouraged her to trust him to decide what was best for her life. He treated his entire congregation with the same manipulation tactics. He abused power to receive finances in order to live the "good life" while members of his congregation sacrificed. He expected them to get by with less and less money and resources while he stockpiled belongings and indulged in a rich lifestyle.

His teachings were close to the truth, using Bible verses to support his claims—but his version of truth was often slightly off the bubble of center. My friend eventually withdrew her church membership and came back to her senses. Now she speaks out about spiritual deception so that others aren't sucked in to similar abuse. She lost years of time with family and friends, because this

> God gives each of us a built-in lie detector through the discernment of the Holy Spirit.

church group isolated her from all she held dear. Even though she's spending every moment now trying to catch up for all the time lost, she knows nothing will ever completely repair what she gave up.

> *We demolish arguments and every pretension that sets itself up against the knowledge of God, and we take captive every thought to make it obedient to Christ.* (2 Corinthians 10:5 NIV)

God gives each of us a built-in lie detector through the discernment of the Holy Spirit. We can filter all teaching through that detector to determine if it contains truth—just as the Bible is truth. Job's friends twisted scriptural truth and applied it the way that best fit their agenda. Their theories about why Job suffered so many trials at once was incorrect—and God proved them wrong. We looked at this Scripture before, but let's look at it in light of this chapter's theme:

> *After the LORD had spoken these words to Job, the LORD said to Eliphaz the Temanite: "My anger burns against you and against your two friends, for you have not spoken of me what is right, as my servant Job has. Now therefore take seven bulls and seven rams and go to my servant Job and offer up a burnt offering for yourselves. And my servant Job shall pray for you,*

for I will accept his prayer not to deal with you according to your folly. For you have not spoken of me what is right, as my servant Job has." So Eliphaz the Temanite and Bildad the Shuhite and Zophar the Naamathite went and did what the LORD had told them, and the LORD accepted Job's prayer. (Job 42:7–9 ESV)

We know from the above verse that God said Job's friends did not speak rightly of God—and because of their false teachings God was angry toward them. Any time we see Eliphaz, Bildad, or Zophar speaking in the Scriptures, we need to remember how God felt about them. They were not truth speakers!

Job's friends thought monetary wealth and good health were signs of God's favor, and a lack of it indicated some sort of sin. I have to wonder if their insights are contained in the Bible, not because they contain good doctrine, but to teach us to be wary of spiritual leaders who twist concepts of faith to fit their own agenda. This is a good time to mention that we should always consider who is speaking in the Bible before we follow their teaching.

> Abusive spiritual leaders often use words of rebuke to accuse and discourage others rather than words that comfort and encourage.

It would be an easy mistake to take some of the verses out of context and teach them as biblical principles when perhaps the words are more an example of what man-made religion looks like. What if we pulled a statement from one of Job's friends and taught it as a viable Bible lesson? We'd be in big trouble! The context proves their thoughts were mixed up, and their advice misled Job.

In Job 4:5 we see Eliphaz belittling Job, telling him he can't even handle trouble. Abusive spiritual leaders often use words of rebuke to accuse and discourage others rather than words that comfort and encourage. Then in Job 4:8 he uses the typical judgmental guilt tactic, essentially saying to Job, "You're reaping what you have sowed." It's always easy for those who deem themselves more spiritual to assume the suffering someone else endures is punishment for sin. Partly, they don't want to think bad things can happen to good people, because that means it could happen to them. And partly, I think it's because they think they are "untouchable."

Often the source of knowledge for an abusive personality is what gets them off track from God and Scripture. Eliphaz relied on a spirit to give him counsel.

> *"Now a word was brought to me stealthily; my ear received the whisper of it. Amid thoughts from visions of the night, when deep sleep falls on men, dread came upon me, and trembling, which made all my bones shake. A spirit glided past my face; the hair of my flesh stood up. It stood still, but I could not discern its appearance. A form was before my eyes; there was silence, then I heard a voice."* (Job 4:12–16 ESV)

It almost sounds like a séance, doesn't it? Creepy!

Bildad based his views on history, tradition, and perhaps in ancestor worship (Job 8:8–10). In Job 20:3, we find that Zophar based his views on his own understanding rather than the teachings of God—sounds a lot like humanism.

The three friends used techniques similar to Satan himself, twisting Scripture to apply in different ways—mixing truth with deception. A spiritual abuser intends to come across sounding pious but will speak partial truths, leaving out essential elements to fit their purposes. In 2 Corinthians 11:14–15 it shows how Satan and his demons can appear as ministers of righteousness. They can sound pretty convincing! But they miss the important application of grace and love—truly misrepresenting the very heart of God.

Job's three friends didn't have a message of redemption and reconciliation with the Lord. They saw God as a cause-and-effect God. If you scratch my back, I'll scratch yours. If you serve me in holiness, I'll bless you with prosperity and health and children. And if I remove blessing, it's because you've reneged on your part of our deal. They believed withdrawal of blessing must mean one had fallen out of favor with God.

There's only one problem with the supposition these friends made of Job—they were wrong. They didn't know his situation—they didn't know fully of his relationship with God. They assumed incorrectly, and when they thought they were speaking for the Lord, they were actually doing the enemy's work.

Some of today's misconceptions being taught in church are similar to the teachings by Job's friends, such as:

- Just serve God, and he will bless you with money and health.

- If you decree a thing, it will come to pass. Claim your new car, and God will park it in your driveway!

- If you would have lived right, you wouldn't have these problems.

- If you had more faith, your sickness would be cured, and your poverty would disappear.

- If you operate in fear, whatever you fear will come to pass.

None of the above principles are biblical, yet they sound so close to truth. That's what false teachers rely on to confuse and convince us. We know Job's friends were wrong. Scripture is very clear that before Job's first calamity ever struck, God esteemed Job highly and didn't put him in the category with the ungodly. He commended Job's faith. He didn't scold Job for a lack of faith.

> There once was a man named Job who lived in the land of Uz. He was blameless—a man of complete integrity. He feared God and stayed away from evil. (Job 1:1)

Then the LORD asked Satan, "Have you noticed my servant Job? He is the finest man in all the earth. He is blameless—a man of complete integrity. He fears God and stays away from evil." (Job 1:8)

Warnings about False Teachers

There are at least three types of false teachers. The first type is *heretics*—those who openly reject the Word of God and teach contrary to it. Others are *apostates*—those who previously followed the faith but have turned away. The trickiest ones to identify are the *deceivers*—those who pretend to align with Christians. They claim to teach biblical truth, yet they teach lies.

1. *"Beware of false prophets, who come to you in sheep's clothing but inwardly are ravenous wolves. You will recognize them by their fruits. Are grapes gathered from thornbushes, or figs from thistles?"* (Matthew 7:15–16 ESV)

2. *But false prophets also arose among the people, just as there will be false teachers among you, who will secretly bring in destructive heresies, even denying the Master who bought them, bringing upon themselves swift destruction.* (2 Peter 2:1 ESV)

3. *For many deceivers have gone out into the world, those who do not confess the coming of Jesus Christ in the flesh. Such a one is the deceiver and the antichrist.* (2 John 7 ESV)

4. *I appeal to you, brothers, to watch out for those who cause divisions and create obstacles contrary to the doctrine that you have been taught; avoid them. For such persons do not serve our Lord Christ, but their own appetites, and by smooth talk and flattery they deceive the hearts of the naive.* (Romans 16:17–18 ESV)

5. *The prophets prophesy falsely, and the priests rule at their direction; my people love to have it so, but what will you do when the end comes?* (Jeremiah 5:31 ESV)

Family Recipes

Ingredients to Discerning Deception

1. **Consult Scripture as your guide to truth.** *Your word is a lamp to my feet and a light to my path* (Psalm 119:105 ESV).

2. **Be in tune to any red flag warnings in your head or heart.** Does the Holy Spirit indwelling within connect with the same spirit in the one you are testing for truth or deception? Or does he reveal a disconnect? Some call this warning signal "a check in my spirit." *Dear friends, do not believe everyone who claims to speak by the Spirit. You must test them to see if the spirit they have comes from God. For there are many false prophets in the world* (1 John 4:1).

3. **Test the content and the methods to determine if they match up to the teachings of Christ.** If the false teacher tries to draw you into his realm of influence, beware. *See to it that no one takes you captive by philosophy and empty deceit, according to human tradition, according to the elemental spirits of the world, and not according to Christ* (Colossians 2:8 ESV).

4. **When you are taught by this leader, check to see if you feel closer to the Lord, or if you are even more confused.** *For God is not a God of confusion but of peace. As in all the churches of the saints* (1 Corinthians 14:33 ESV).

5. **False leaders often manipulate with smooth-talking charisma to get what they want.** *And now I make one more appeal, my dear brothers and sisters. Watch out for people who cause divisions and upset people's faith by teaching things contrary to what you have been taught. Stay away from them. Such people are not serving Christ our Lord; they are serving their own personal interests. By smooth talk and glowing words they deceive innocent people* (Romans 16:17–18).

6. **Deceptive, prideful leaders motivate you to follow them rather than spotlighting Christ from a position of humility and submission.** *Jesus told him, "I am the way, the truth, and the life. No one can come to the Father except through me"* (John 14:6).

To Ponder

*   How does the leader use Scripture to teach their version of truth? How does their teaching compare to Bible truths?

*   What are the perceived goals of the leader?

*   Does the leader reflect Christ-like virtues and spiritual fruit, or does he appear to have self-centered motives? Is he self-indulgent while expecting others to sacrifice?

*   Does the teacher use manipulation tactics and guilt trips to motivate listeners?

*   Am I at peace or experiencing confusion and chaos when I'm under this leader's authority?

*   Does this spiritual leader use methods of teaching that create an abuse of power and control?

Instructions for Living

1. If you are currently in a church or relationship with abusive tendencies, pray and ask God what he wants you to do. If you are not currently in a relationship that uses faith as a manipulation tactic, you probably know someone who is—or someone who is recovering from one. Be in prayer for them and for you. This is one of those situations where we can agree, "There but for the grace of God, go I."

2. Believers have a hard time leaving a church or a relationship founded on their faith, because they want to remain humble

and yielded. So it's important to realize if God leads you to exit, it's not a self-centered decision. It's a healthy choice to get you to a better place for your spiritual needs.

3. If God leads you to stay, ask him to show you healthier insights and boundaries. It's possible God wants you to be a part of the remnant of truth left in the church, used by him to intervene and create accountability for the deceptive leaders. Sometimes we give a faith leader more power and control than they need to have in our lives, because we buckle under their pressure. They know which buttons to push in us to get us to respond the way they want us to respond. So be on guard for their tactics.

Questions

Note: When I ask about your involvement with a spiritual leader in the following questions, I mean it in the broadest sense. It could be a spouse who uses religious teachings for control, pastors, deacons, or other church members—any powerful person who uses twisted teachings on God and Scripture to manipulate you or someone you know. Others in this definition include employers, supervisors, and those in Christian media (authors, television personalities, and those who have radio programs). Anyone who has the opportunity to mislead you.

•   Have you been previously wounded by a spiritual leader? How long did it take to wise up to the error of their ways? What was your biggest struggle with it?

•   Are you currently going through a trial caused by a spiritual leader? What is your biggest struggle with it?

•   What advice would you tell a friend who's going through a situation like that today?

•   How can we guard our own views of Scripture and God to make sure we do not use our beliefs to deceive others?

Family Legacy

Pass these values to the next generation in your families—your biological family as well as your spiritual family. Mentor them by teaching the following truths so they can avoid being deceived and determine not to be a deceiver to others.

1. **Surround yourself with godly people to steer clear of going down the wrong path in life.** *Do not be so deceived and misled! Evil companionships (communion, associations) corrupt and deprave good manners and morals and character* (1 Corinthians 15:33 AMPC).

2. **Avoid partnering with someone who doesn't share your same faith values, especially when it comes to important decisions.** *Don't team up with those who are unbelievers. How can righteousness be a partner with wickedness? How can light live with darkness?* (2 Corinthians 6:14).

3. **Turn from others who are puffed up by their own version of wisdom. Escaping evil will refresh you and heal your wounds.** *Be not wise in your own eyes; fear the LORD, and turn away from evil. It will be healing to your flesh and refreshment to your bones* (Proverbs 3:7–8 ESV).

4. **When you teach, be sure not to stray from the true message of the Bible passage.** *Do your best to present yourself to God as one approved, a worker who has no need to be ashamed, rightly handling the word of truth* (2 Timothy 2:15 ESV).

5. **Be genuine in your own faith walk.** *So that the tested genuineness of your faith—more precious than gold that perishes though it is tested by fire—may be found to result in praise and glory and honor at the revelation of Jesus Christ* (1 Peter 1:7 ESV).

6. **Share your previous experience of spiritual abuse with someone who is currently dealing with a toxic church or false teacher, and show them how God rescued you from it,**

so that they might hope again. *But in your hearts revere Christ as Lord. Always be prepared to give an answer to everyone who asks you to give the reason for the hope that you have. But do this with gentleness and respect* (1 Peter 3:15 NIV).

7. **If a relationship with someone of influence induces fear or confusion in you, recognize this as a mind-control technique. God will never lead someone to attempt to control you.** *For God has not given us a spirit of fear, but of power and of love and of a sound mind* (2 Timothy 1:7 NKJV). *For God is not* the author *of confusion but of peace, as in all the churches of the saints* (1 Corinthians 14:33 NKJV). *For where envy and self-seeking* exist, *confusion and every evil thing* are *there* (James 3:16 NKJV).

Prayer Intervention

If someone you love is involved in a spiritually abusive relationship at home or church, the first line of defense is prayer.

Pray for:

- Wisdom, direction and knowledge.

- Victims who have been physically, emotionally, or spiritually wounded by abusers.

- Healing to those experiencing anger, bitterness, and unforgiveness because of painful spiritual abuse.

- God's comfort and healing to soothe the burdens of those harmed by spiritual deception.

- Clarity of thought based on Scripture and Holy Spirit discernment for those confused by the false teachings of others.

- Those who have turned away from God because of these spiritual abusers, that they will turn back to God and find a teacher of biblical truth.

- Those who are against "organized religion" due to exposure to a toxic church experience, that they will be open to what the Bible teaches and find a healthy church environment.

- Those who have left Christianity due to a false teacher, that they will see the truth and come back.

- Those seeking a religion, that they will instead find a relationship with the Lord Jesus Christ, so that expectations are aligned with Bible teaching rather than unbiblical traditions and rules.

Family Chat

Have you had a painful wound caused by an "upstanding" church member? How many of us have been nearly slaughtered by another church member? It hurts *more* coming from a fellow church member, because we expect better of them—we expect them to love us the way we want to be loved. And when they do the exact opposite of that—how can we feel free to worship with our church family anymore? It's hard, and there are no pat answers!

> God has not let me down one single time.

One time, I posted a thought on Facebook about God's amazing attributes. One of my school friends commented that she didn't want to have anything to do with church, because her Christian friends had wounded her deeply. She said it, thinking I would defend them because they were Christians. Instead, I surprised her by responding this way:

"I'm so sorry that happened to you. I can relate a little bit. All of the lowest spots in my life involved being hurt by people claiming the Christian label. Sometimes they just didn't know better. They were unaware of my needs. They treated me like I was invisible. But sometimes, it went beyond them letting me down. It was spiritual abuse. Christian bullies. The post I made though, wasn't about Christians, it was about God. And God has not let me down one single time. His comfort and compassion. His mercy and grace. His peace and his strength. They are what get me through. Every. Single. Day.

"Russ and I have changed into people with hearts for *all* people. We are a lot different than what you might think. I would like to hope we could offer you some compassion. Russ works as a hospice chaplain and helps those who the rest of the world has counted out. And we both have others visit our home who feel like misfits and outcasts. Because really, aren't we all, in some way or another? It's not about checking off a list of dos and don'ts. It's not about rules and regulations. It's about doing life together in relationship with each other and with God. It's about noticing the struggles as much as the successes. I can honestly say I have met others who love God and love people and truly make a difference."

My schoolmate and I still have a relationship, because she felt heard and seen by me. If I had given her a flippant reply that minimized her wound, she would have tuned me out. Now she thanks me for my prayers.

> Our best defense to deception is to know what the Bible says.

This interaction reminded me of a quote by Madeleine L'Engle. "We draw people to Christ not by loudly discrediting what they believe, by telling them how wrong they are and how right we are, but by showing them a light that is so lovely that they want with all their hearts to know the source of it."

One caution for all of us who have been hurt by a church situation: we are more likely to be attracted to a church environment that is radically different from what we have experienced before. But in so doing, we could easily follow a leader who has strayed from biblical application. We need to be watchful of the fellowship in which we join.

It is good for us to seek peace in the church. Harmony and unity are so important for our witness in the community and for our ministry to all who enter in to worship with us. Let us pray for our church leaders to have wisdom when dealing with division and destructive behavior in the church.

Our best defense to deception is to know what the Bible says. When you read Scripture, pray for God to give you understanding of his Word. This knowledge will give you the discernment you need to know when a Bible teacher or church leader strays from truth. Knowing what God says in Scripture is the number one way to prevent being deceived.

Closing Prayer

Lord God who leads with grace, help me to have discernment with any leaders using Scripture with authority. Show me what I need to see. Direct me if you want me to get out of the situation or if you want me to speak up. Also, help me as I lead others, so that I do not manipulate biblical principles to fit a personal agenda. Comfort hearts and heal wounds as only you can. Amen.

Chapter Five

WHEN I'M DISAPPOINTED

While there's not much mention of it in Job, we can see that he was frustrated by his remaining relationships after his children all died on the same day. It's safe to say he dealt with unmet and unrealistic expectations with his wife and friends. In this chapter we'll address the hurts that hit closest to home—those inflicted on us by, or because of, the ones we love most. We'll deal with these disappointments, learn to adjust our expectations of others, and help them adjust their expectations of us.

Family Album

Hair Today, Gone Tomorrow?

We women obsess about our hair. Finding a good hair stylist is similar to finding our mates for life. The search can bring about several one-date wonders on the journey toward connection. We want a stylist who understands our every desire: an easy style that is not only trendy but also face-flattering. We expect them to do magic with our uncooperative hair. And many of us also want them to be color artists. They are often the supplier of the "fix" for our chemically dependent hair.

The best way to find the perfect stylist is to find someone with a hairstyle you like and ask them which salon they frequent. When I complimented my friend Brooke about her new 'do, she referred me to Daniel. She said he was worth the trip out of town and gave me his number. I also liked the new hairstyle on my friend Linda, and she said she went to Daniel and gave me the address. I figured if two of my girlfriends like Daniel, he must be good.

I made my appointment and drove to Carlsbad, but Daniel said I wasn't on his shedule. After doing some investigation I discovered Brooke's Daniel was in the opposite direction, in Roswell. There were actually three Daniels who style hair! Disappointed and deflated, I rescheduled. Sometimes when we are desperate for something, we end up jumping to the wrong conclusions. I made the mistake of assuming these two stylists were the same guy.

Finally, the new appointment date arrived on my calendar. I made certain to get the address correct and ventured to the different town. This time, nothing would get between me and my hair's new style. I enjoyed my first "date" with him so much, I made an appointment for a total hair redo. My biggest hair adventure ever—foils! Again, I waited for the day, as if marking off dates on the Advent calendar prior to Christmas.

On my special renovation day, I jetted off to Roswell. During the drive, I daydreamed about my potential new look. Anticipation caused me to bolt out of the car into the salon. But to my dismay, Daniel was not in. He called in sick and couldn't reach me to reschedule. I had traveled forty-five minutes from Artesia for this? Others would have severed the relationship at that point, but not me. I was in pursuit of the perfect hairstyle. It was merely postponed—not out of reach. I rescheduled *again*, and when I next met Daniel, we finally got it right. It was a hair partnership to "dye" for.

Yes, I realize all this talk about hair is much ado about nothing. But first impressions and the opinions of others matters to us. *"People judge by outward appearance, but the LORD looks at the heart"* (1 Samuel 16:7).

Others can't help but think of us based partly on what they see. They do not have the ability to read our minds or see into our hearts, so they study our physical appearance and our disposition.

1 Corinthians 11 says our hair is our glory. It represents our surrendered will to God. Hair is a woman's covering. The word *covering* in the Bible often represented a believer's prayer position before God. Hair said a lot in biblical times, and it says a lot today.

Sometimes all the brouhaha lives up to our expectations, and other times it doesn't. Daniel, *Brooke's* Daniel, did not disappoint!

Family Bible

Read the entire chapter of Job 17. Job is speaking—his heart bleeding through these words. Friends, loved ones, and religious leaders had hurt him so much. He was disappointed in how they treated him. He expected them to be there for him, and they weren't. Look especially at these phrases from the New Living Translation of Job 17. We see how he felt about his relationships—and in general.

- *My spirit is crushed, and my life is nearly snuffed out* (v. 1).

- *I am surrounded by mockers. I watch how bitterly they taunt me* (v. 2).

- *No one else will stand up for me* (v. 3).

- *They betray their friends for their own advantage* (v. 5).

- *God has made a mockery of me among the people; they spit in my face* (v. 6).

- *My eyes are swollen with weeping* (v. 7).

- *As for all of you, come back with a better argument, though I still won't find a wise man among you* (v. 10).

- *My hopes have disappeared. My heart's desires are broken* (v. 11).

- *These men say that night is day; they claim that the darkness is light* (v. 12).

- *Where then is my hope? Can anyone find it?* (v. 15).

David Also Dealt with People Disappointing Him

David was disheartened by his enemies' motives and actions—they tried (on purpose) to hurt him.

> *I will shout for joy and sing your praises, for you have ransomed me. I will tell about your righteous deeds all day long, for everyone who tried to hurt me has been shamed and humiliated.* (Psalm 71:23–24)

What about us? Can we react like David? Even before our bad situations start to reverse, can we praise the Lord? Can we say with David:

- My lips shout for joy.

- I sing praises to God.

- I rejoice because my soul has been redeemed, rescued, and ransomed by God.

- All day long I'll speak of his righteous deeds.

> *For am I now seeking the approval of man, or of God? Or am I trying to please man? If I were still trying to please man, I would not be a servant of Christ.* (Galatians 1:10 ESV)

It must have disappointed Job to do all he did (even making sacrifices on behalf of his children) and have others not come through when he needed them. If anyone had a right to ask, "After all I've done for you—you treat me *this* way?" it was Job. This passage from Galatians helps us realize it's human nature to be people pleasers. But to be a true servant of Christ, we have to let go of our expectations of self and others and serve God alone.

> Even before our bad situations start to reverse, can we praise the Lord?

Colossians 3:2 (ESV) says, *Set your minds on things that are above, not on things that are on earth.* Let go of the old ways of doing life, and pursue him alone. In 2 Corinthians 5:17 (ESV) we are told, *Therefore, if anyone is in Christ, he is a new creation. The old has passed away; behold, the new has come.* What can we do in a new way when it comes to being disappointed by others? We can handle it differently, knowing God has equipped us with a new way to deal with our struggles. We abide in him and have access to nearly all his resources.

One way to discover a new way to handle our hurts is to concentrate on a new mindset. Let's point our focus where we want our hearts and minds to go.

- *For those who live according to the flesh set their minds on the things of the flesh, but those who live according to the Spirit set their minds on the things of the Spirit.* (Romans 8:5 esv)

- *And so, dear brothers and sisters, I plead with you to give your bodies to God because of all he has done for you. Let them be a living and holy sacrifice—the kind he will find acceptable. This is truly the way to worship him. Don't copy the behavior and customs of this world, but let God transform you into a new person by changing the way you think. Then you will learn to know God's will for you, which is good and pleasing and perfect.* (Romans 12:1–2)

- *And be constantly renewed in the spirit of your mind [having a fresh mental and spiritual attitude].* (Ephesians 4:23 AMPC)

Learning from David's Expectations

We can learn about dealing with expectations from David. Samuel anointed David king of Israel, but he was not given the throne right away. During his wait, he spent years fleeing from the murderous agenda of a jealous and vindictive (not to mention unstable) King Saul. David expected to be Israel's new leader, but his reality for quite some time was that of a runaway.

> Let's point our focus where we want our hearts and minds to go.

David could have been disappointed when his real life didn't measure up to his expectations. He could have blamed Samuel and even God for not fulfilling their promises to him. Talk about unmet expectations! But it seems as if David used the time while retreating from Saul to retreat in other ways too. He somehow reframed his expectations and made sure his heart aligned with the heart of God. In Psalm 62:1 (ESV) he wrote, *For God alone my soul waits in silence; from him comes my salvation.* He managed to be patient in his wait, knowing he only needed to pursue God. In Psalm 62:5 (ESV) it says, *For God alone, O my soul, wait in silence, for my hope is from him.*

Not only did David realign his expectations, but he made sure the object of his hope was also God alone. By anchoring his hope to God's promises, he was equipped to wait for the right timing and not try to take matters into his own hands. Human nature would have motivated most of us to get ahead of God and force the situation, using our own abilities to get what we figured we had coming to us.

Any time we base our expectations on something outside our

control, we are setting ourselves up for disappointment. Our bank accounts can change. Our family structure isn't set in stone. Even where we live or work or worship can be different during various seasons of our lives. If we invest our hopes and happiness in the promises or commitments of someone else, there's always a risk of having our hearts broken.

Instead, like David, we need to place our hope squarely in the Lord alone.

Learning from John's Expectations

Read Matthew 11:1–6 and consider John's expectations of Jesus. It's possible John the Baptist expected Jesus to be cut from the same cloth as he was. Hellfire and brimstone, locust and honey and loincloths. A voice in the wilderness. He expected Jesus to instantly be both judge and king. But Jesus wasn't John. The truth is, we're all different, and we can't expect others to handle life stuff the same way we do. There's no one right way to react or respond.

> By anchoring our hope to God's promises we are equipped to wait for the right timing.

When John was in prison, he sent some of his followers to ask Jesus, *"Are you the one who is to come, or shall we look for another?"* (Matthew 11:3 ESV). Maybe he was questioning his expectations of the Savior at that point. Jesus didn't chastise John for asking. He can handle our questions. We can take our unmet expectations to him, whether they concern him directly or indirectly.

Jesus answered by highlighting all of his great works and miracles. We can learn from that how important perspective is to deal with our disappointments. If we are so focused on our unmet expectations, we will miss out on seeing God at work around us. Jesus reminded John of all these divine appointments. Often we need to allow Jesus the opportunity to remind us of what he's been doing while we've been fixated on our problems. How much better to make a list of the blessings than to list our frustrations and disappointments. Just like John reached out to Jesus when he began to question, we need to draw closer to the Lord during our trials and unwanted circumstances.

Family Recipes

Ingredients for Resolution

It's a fact of life, others will let us down. Because we want God's best for them, it hurts when they choose a different way. What should we do?

1. **Still love them.** Sometimes we're more in love with the idea of loving them than we're committed to making the relationships work. We don't have to love their attitudes or actions, and we don't even have to *like* the person right then! Continue to hope they will realign more with God's principles.

2. **Show truth and light through love.** Ask God how to show them his love rather than praying they respond according to our agenda. Evaluate, what does God want from this? How can we release our feelings so our emotions don't compound the problem? How can we be okay if this is never resolved to our satisfaction? It's not about us. It's about reflecting God's light even when others don't care to stand in that light.

3. **Discern what is toxic and when it's time for tough love.** It's wise to ask God how involved we should be with others who aren't a positive part of our lives. Maybe they create a toxic response in us. It's healthy to avoid getting too close with others who don't have a priority of faith in their lives. And if a believer has made it a practice to oppose godly principles, ask God if it's time to practice tough love, as hard as that is.

4. **Choose when to draw the line.** No matter what we do, it's outside our control when the other person goes off course. All we have control over is our response and the way we deal with our feelings. We can choose to discontinue doing favors for these toxic ones if they treat us poorly.

5. **Release them to God.** Love doesn't mean we roll over and play dead. It means we release them, much like the prodigal son, to find their way back to what God wants in their lives. It also means being willing to receive them back when they come with repentant hearts.

6. **Keep a proper focus.** Avoid getting worked up about their faults and flaws. Choose not to focus on their self-absorption, distorted perspectives, or poor communications skills. Often the very thing we get frustrated about in someone else is something we need to work on too. Use their dysfunction as a mirror—to reveal what needs to be adjusted in our own lives.

Your Reactions Are Showing

Our expectations of how others respond to us are usually based on how we think we would respond in the same situation—we expect them to have our same standard operating

> Sometimes we're more in love with the idea of loving them than we're committed to making the relationships work.

system. And selfishly, we build up these expectations based on what we want to see happen to benefit our own agendas. Often our expectations aren't realistic, and that's how we end up with unmet expectations. This leads to disappointment in the relationship and disappointment in the other party.

Unfulfilled promises cause disappointment. The more others let us down, the more guarded we are with new interactions. We think we can mitigate future frustrations and disappointments by being less involved in our relationships. As we attempt to avoid new messes, our relationships become shallow and insincere.

We gain wisdom and perspective as we seek God's principles for our relationships. God our Creator knows what makes us tick (and what makes the other person tick too!). Let's look to him for advice on developing healthier relationships. He will inspire us to go on even when we manage to mess things up or they hurt us—again.

To Ponder

- Why do I put so much importance on how others treat me?

- Do I seek the approval of others more than I seek the Lord?

- When I'm rejected or brushed off by others, do I react as God would have me to respond?

- Do I neglect the relationships God has entrusted to me?

- Do I communicate truth in a way that prevents incorrect assumptions and unrealistic expectations? How I can I improve the way I communicate to avoid misunderstandings?

- How can I show *love* when I don't *like* what they're doing?

Instructions for Living

When your relationships disappoint you, there are five important things you can do:

1. **Don't give in to disappointment.** The enemy loves for us to be ineffective for Christ due to our relationship frustrations. Determine not to listen to the attitude of defeat. Instead, focus on how God is making a difference in your life. It might be a lesson to learn, a new friend to discover, a change of heart. And it might be that you are right where God wants you— where someone *else* can see your example.

2. **Lean in to your relationship with God.** Allow prayer and mditation to be an intimate give-and-take discussion with the Father. When you turn to him rather than to your other life-savers, you've found true contentment. He wants to rescue us from our everyday devastations—not just our once-in-a-life-time hurts.

3. **Help others—take the focus off of self for a while.** When the task is complete, you might find you have a new attitude.

4. **Allow the unmet expectations to help build endurance in you.** *Be assured* and *understand that the trial* and *proving of your faith bring out endurance* and *steadfastness* and *patience* (James 1:3 AMPC).

5. **When life is tumultuous, seek the kind of peace that supersedes all the disappointments.** *Don't worry about anything; instead, pray about everything. Tell God what you need, and thank him for all he has done. Then you will experience God's peace, which exceeds anything we can understand. His peace will guard your hearts and minds as you live in Christ Jesus* (Philippians 4:6–7).

Questions

- What do you need to add to your prayers to prevent worry (anxiety)? What do you need to tell God? What will he do for you when you've done all this?

- How might you adjust your expectations in others, so you aren't hurt as often when they don't measure up to your hopes for them?

- Other than communication flaws, what other elements cause expectations to be more trying than usual?

- Are you experiencing a toxic relationship? What can you do about it?

- How do you handle stressful relationship situations when you have no control over the outcome?

Family Legacy

We can pass along to the next generation what we have learned about interacting with others, so they don't repeat some of our same mistakes. Our loved ones and friends need to know we care about them. We can live out some of these relationship principles in such a way so others learn how to have fewer unrealistic and unmet expectations.

Avoid Relationship Messes

There's something to be said for lowering our standards! Let God be the one to set up the rules and regulations in the lives of others. We have a hard enough time living up to the rules and regs God gives *us* to accomplish, let alone policing the successes and failures of others.

> We're setting ourselves up for disappointment when we rely on others for our positive attitudes.

Sometimes we are going to be hurt. That's simply a fact of life. Others let us down. It's up to us to decide if our expectations are unrealistic. If we're being unfair in what we hope others say and do, we need to back off our expectations. Sometimes our expectations are reasonable and in line with Scripture. When they chose to go a different way, then we need to let our feelings be less affected by their choices. Sure, we will feel something. We're human. But we get a choice how long we allow those feelings to be hurt or disappointed. Any time their actions and reactions are outside our control, we need to make sure our joy is not based on their choices. We're setting ourselves up for disappointment when we rely on others for our positive attitudes.

We also get hurt when we don't meet *their* unrealistic expectations.

We don't like to let people down! It's easy to feel judged a failure when this happens. The best way to handle it is to ask God and the one we let down to show us what we need to do to make things right. We have the opportunity to strive to do better when it's in our power and ability to do so. If what they want is unfounded, then it's time to communicate why we can't measure up to their expectations.

It's too difficult to try to live up to the attitudes, actions, and conversations all the others want from us. We can simplify our lives and reduce stress when we focus on the agenda God has for us rather than the agenda others have. We can't please everyone—and some days, we're lucky to please ourselves!

Questions We Ask

- How can I seek comfort in God alone (and not people)?

- How can I avoid linking my happiness to how someone else acts or responds?

- Do I have a right to my feelings when someone else hurts me?

- How can I avoid frustration when their choices hurt me?

- How can I trust someone when I have to lower my expectations because of their poor choices and actions?

- When is it time to pull out of a relationship, and when is it healthy to resolve it?

Rules for Improved Relationships

1. Realize a loving relationship with someone is more important than just about anything, including winning a disagreement. When we pursue showing we are right more than we pursue showing love to others, it will lead to disappointment.

2. Forgiveness is vital to resolving conflict. It doesn't mean bailing someone out when they mess up or getting defensive when being judged. It means giving each other a fresh start.

3. Your love for someone will grow the more you pray for them and seek God's best for their lives.

4. To show love more, try these *others-focused* gestures: show concern, ask about them, be interested in their interests, look to supply for their real needs.

5. It's not your job to try to fix everything. It's your job to love them even when they feel unloved or unlovable. Maybe some things are outside your control for a reason.

6. Agree to disagree agreeably.

Communication Techniques

Try this phrasing the next time you need to bring up an unpleasant topic with someone you care about. It puts the failure on you (your struggle) and allows the recipient of the critique to hear what they need to improve without feeling attacked or getting defensive.

> *I'm having a struggle. Can we talk about it? I have a hard time when you _____ because it makes me feel _____. I don't want it to be that way and hope we can talk it out.*

Another technique to avoid misunderstandings is to listen to what they want to tell you and then say back to them:

> *What I'm hearing you say is _____. Am I understanding you correctly or did you mean something else?*

Elements to Misunderstandings

Often our stress exacerbates misunderstandings. Be aware of the following elements in your life and in the lives of those you love. When these stressors are in action, it's more likely for a conflict to arise. This is the time to release the other person from any sort of expectations until they have time to heal from being overwhelmed.

Relationship Stressors:

- Fatigue
- Deadlines
- Pressure elsewhere
- Self-loathing
- Guilt feelings from unconfessed sin
- Feeling fragile (overly sensitive)

Legacy Builders

1. **You can't handle life alone. Friends are a necessity.** You might be disappointed by your friends and family, but don't give up trying to have relationships. *A person standing alone can be attacked and defeated, but two can stand back-to-back and conquer. Three are even better, for a triple-braided cord is not easily broken* (Ecclesiastes 4:12).

2. **Evaluate if your expectations are realistic.** Use wisdom and discernment in your dealings with others. *Teach me good judgment, wise* and *right discernment, and knowledge, for I have believed (trusted, relied on, and clung to) Your commandments* (Psalm 119:66 AMPC).

3. **Your pain is never wasted.** God will use it to help you help others during their time of need. *All praise to God, the Father of our Lord Jesus Christ. God is our merciful Father and the source of all comfort. He comforts us in all our troubles so that we can comfort others. When they are troubled, we will be able to give them the same comfort God has given us* (2 Corinthians 1:3–4).

Family Chat

Sometimes we find others interesting because they are different. They intrigue us. That whole opposites attract thing. We have to remind ourselves those very differences also mean they will respond differently than we do. How many times do we feel hurt because of something they said or did (or *didn't* say or do), and there was no intent from the other party to wound us? They simply didn't think through how it would affect us.

Other people are going through their own trials. How they interact with us (or avoid us) may have nothing to do with us. Remind yourself they might merely be trying to survive their own hardships—it isn't intentional neglect. Worse, when we build a wall to protect ourselves from perceived hurt, we prevent ourselves from being available to them as they go through their crisis. We think our relationship *is* the crisis.

> We aren't designed or equipped to face trials alone—we all need support.

Walls isolate us from anyone being able to help us when we're hurting and keep us from truly seeing what others are going through. Walls divide and create islands. We're on our own to fight our battles. We aren't designed or equipped to face trials alone—we all need support. We separate ourselves from others to avoid pain. This creates a recipe to feel overwhelmed, because we're trying to handle life all alone. The barriers we create often are responsible for the pain and disappointment we experience.

One way we can deal with unmet or unrealistic expectations is to put our thoughts in the proper perspective. Often we don't take the time to do that. We're more interested in our feelings being hurt, getting what we think we deserve, or something not being right or fair. In other words, we don't outgrow thinking like two-year-olds! When we do something over and over without trying to proceed in a new or different way, we are setting ourselves up for failure and disappointment. But we do it anyway. Why? Because it's human nature. And the only way to fight human nature is by using the fruit and gifts of the Spirit.

Sometimes we play the what-if game. We ask ourselves how we

think a situation with someone else will play out. Then we allow every worst-case scenario to run through our minds. And we ask, "Why are they treating me this way?" We make assumptions. We can sure mess up our relationships, can't we?

Sandy Bassett mentioned an interesting phenomenon about how we compare what we would do to how others act in the same situation. She said, "We conjure up our ideal response—the model attitudes and actions we would have. But if we were actually put in those situations, this ideal response is not typically what occurs." We allow ourselves time to come up with the perfect response or reaction, when in actuality the person we believe failed the test had to respond and react on the spot with no time to think it through. Anyone can pass the test when it's an "open book" test. It's when we are tested on the fly that we find out if we really know how we will act!

> Take a step back from your relationship in the physical sense, but take a step forward in praying for them.

We need to give others the freedom to respond in their way—not our way. This releases expectations and allows for living life un-conditionally. Sometimes we have to take a step back from a rela-tionship in the physical sense, but take a step forward in praying for them.

Closing Prayer

Father, I often have more questions than answers. More hurts than remedies. In honesty, I bring to you the frustrations of my heart. I'm overwhelmed. Stressed. Yes, even licking my wounds at times rather than letting hurts go. I can't do life on my own. Equip me with what I need to survive these relationship disappointments. Sometimes I can walk away from unhealthy friendships, and sometimes I'm related to the ones who make me feel so neglected or agitated. Tear down my walls—the walls I build to hide from you—and the walls I put up to avoid others. I even barricade my own heart and mind to try to dull the pain. Knock them all down. Show me the relationships in which you want me to invest my time and emotion. Let it begin in my time and honest dialogue with you. Amen.

Chapter Six

WHEN I'M DISABLED

Not only did Job lose his relationships, he lost his health. He suffered excruciating symptoms, and when he needed the comfort of others the most, they ostracized him. Anyone who deals with acute or chronic health conditions can relate. Learn new coping skills as you suffer, and allow yourself to grieve the loss of your health. Then, with a healthy perspective, reach out to others who are enduring similar afflictions.

Family Album

Top Ten Alternatives to "I'm Fine"

I've had chronic health problems for thirty years and find it gets old to answer the question "How are you?" Most people don't really want to know, and most days I don't feel like going into detail anyway. It's far too depressing, boring, and all those other *–ing* words. Yet, at the same time "I'm fine" isn't a truthful statement. I rarely feel fine. Rather than lie, I've come up with these top ten ways to answer the question "How are you?"

1. Ask me after I've had more caffeine!

2. From here up, I'm doing great (on a bad day I point to my chin)!

3. Not bad by my standards.

4. Better than yesterday!

5. I'm excited about (fill-in-the-blank).

6. Hanging in there.

7. Fair to middlin'.

8. Better than that other guy.

9. Not too shabby.

10. Could be better, could be worse.

I realize that most people who ask, "How are you?" are being polite. It's a formality. A greeting. It's not really an open invitation to tell them about my latest medical struggle. If you're not prepared to hear a detailed medical update, it can be a real downer to listen to someone else go on and on about their personal ailment or current tribulation in life.

A friend of mine grinned and said this is called an "organ recital" when a person complains about heart, kidneys, lungs, etc. Some people enjoy the woe-is-me attention of being a martyr. I don't want to burden others with my story unless they want to know.

Since most others don't need a long-winded, depressing description of my diagnosis-du-jour, I don't go into details unless they ask, "How are you—really?" Or they say they are praying for me and want an update. I'd rather focus on whatever good is going on, without sounding like bragging (that too, can be annoying!). When you're not feeling well, what's your "Fine, thank you" reply?

One thing I've learned is that we are three-part beings. The physical is only one-third of the equation. If body, soul, and spirit all get a vote in how I feel, the body loses the vote. So when I do say "I'm fine," I'm technically correct if my soul and spirit are having a good day! They get the majority vote.

Mammogram/Laugh-O-Gram

I'm never more aware of how unique I am than when I go for a mammogram. I was born with a congenital anomaly and have had several surgeries for various conditions. I'll never forget one of my mammo dates. The radiology technician asked the normal questions, but she struggled with my unusual replies. She tried to figure it out, but it wasn't until I disrobed that she understood.

To alleviate her uneasiness, I employed humor as a stress reliever. While she positioned me, I asked if I was her first bionic woman. Not metal, but scars. I was anatomically incorrect. She told me to hold my breath, and then she did too. So I implemented more humor.

> May you have a divine appointment to cheer an invisible sufferer, and may your apprehension be turned to laughter.

I told her we wouldn't want to all look like Barbie dolls. Besides, Barbie had a terrible life. She couldn't get Ken to commit to a marriage, even though she already had the wedding gown. And she couldn't hold down a job—hence career-themed Barbie as a teacher, as a flight attendant, as a doctor . . . you get my drift. I had her in stitches. I broke the ice!

The tech shared with me that she had a congenital abnormality too—pyloric stenosis (meaning food didn't get to her stomach). She hated the huge surgical scar from infancy, which seemed to grow with her.

I comforted her with another dose of humor. "Why is it that some women are blessed with dainty little scars that fade with time, and others of us are cursed with thick red ropes of scar tissue that makes us feel like Frankenstein's Bride?"

"It's such a relief to know I'm not the only one," she sighed.

> Life rarely is limited to one trial at a time. We collect them.

Before I left the room that day, I gave her a hug and reassured her that true beauty comes from within. No one is perfect, except one, and he came as our Savior.

She thanked me for the inspiration. I saw *hope* in her face. I went in apprehensive and left feeling like it was a divine appointment.

May you have a divine appointment to cheer an invisible sufferer, and may your apprehension be turned to laughter.

Family Bible

Satan unleashed a second challenge to test Job—a physical ailment (Job 2:7–13). Medical experts who have read the following passages believe Job was stricken with black leprosy: Job 2:8; 7:4–5; 13:14; 13:28; 16:16; 16:8; 17:1; 19:20; 19:26; 30:17; 30:30. The disease produces swollen arms and legs, itching, skin flaking, skin discoloring, and intense pain. Because the patients look like elephants or lions the disease is sometimes called Elephantiasis or Leontiasis. It changed Job's physical appearance—his friends didn't recognize him (Job 2:12). It affected every part of Job's body. Infection spread from the soles of his feet to the top of his head. He couldn't find a moment's rest from this disease (Job 3:26; 30:17).

He scraped his skin with broken pottery shards (perhaps to debride the skin or because it itched). His skin endured a cyclical attack of decay, hardening, and then breaking out once again (Job 7:5). Job faced physical suffering at a time when his whole world seemed to be falling apart. Often, those who deal with health problems feel the same way. Life rarely is limited to one trial at a time. We collect them.

Why Does God Allow Suffering?

This difficult question has been around almost as long as life itself: "If God is so good, and if he is all-powerful, why does he allow suffering?" We know God is good. *The light shines in the darkness, and the darkness has not overcome it* (John 1:5 ESV). And God is all-powerful. *O Sovereign LORD! You made the heavens and earth by your strong hand and powerful arm. Nothing is too hard for you!* (Jeremiah 32:17).

He is able to prevent suffering or reverse it when it starts, and he is certainly compassionate—it breaks his heart when he sees us in any sort of spiritual, mental, emotional, or physical pain. So why does God allow us to be afflicted? We may never know until the day it doesn't matter anymore—the day we shall endure no more pain. But until then, perhaps we are asking the wrong questions.

When Adam sinned, sin entered the world. Adam's sin brought death, so death spread to everyone, for everyone sinned. (Romans 5:12)

But there is a great difference between Adam's sin and God's gracious gift. For the sin of this one man, Adam, brought death to many. But even greater is God's wonderful grace and his gift of forgiveness to many through this other man, Jesus Christ. And the result of God's gracious gift is very different from the result of that one man's sin. For Adam's sin led to condemnation, but God's free gift leads to our being made right with God, even though we are guilty of many sins. For the sin of this one man, Adam, caused death to rule over many. But even greater is God's wonderful grace and his gift of righteousness, for all who receive it will live in triumph over sin and death through this one man, Jesus Christ. Yes,

> *Adam's one sin brings condemnation for everyone, but Christ's one act of righteousness brings a right relationship with God and new life for everyone.* (Romans 5:15–18)

Adam and Eve made a choice outside God's will, and all of humanity continues to pay the consequences. Rebelling against God is what introduced pain and suffering into the world. It's hard to understand why God allows it, but his perspective is different than ours. He sees the rest of the 3-G story—all about the *gospel* of Christ, God's *goodwill* to humanity, and the *glory* to come.

> *Against its will, all creation was subjected to God's curse. But with eager hope, the creation looks forward to the day when it will join God's children in glorious freedom from death and decay. For we know that all creation has been groaning as in the pains of childbirth right up to the present time.* (Romans 8:20–22)

It's important to note that even though pain isn't caused by a person's sin, it's a general principle. As long as sin is in the world, humans will face suffering. Each person who endures illness and affliction isn't stricken due to personal sin, but due to the consequences of sin on all of humanity. Job's friends believed suffering was a direct result of a person's unconfessed sin. Why? If it were true, as long as they lived up to the right standards, they might avoid such severe suffering. Jesus vehemently refuted this sort of teaching about physical disorders.

To complicate matters, we know that sometimes in Scripture a person *does* suffer as a consequence of rebelling against God. But evidently it's not the *only* reason people suffer.

> *As Jesus was walking along, he saw a man who had been blind from birth. "Rabbi," his disciples asked him, "why was this man born blind? Was it because of his own sins or his parents' sins?"*

"It was not because of his sins or his parents' sins," Jesus answered. "This happened so the power of God could be seen in him." (John 9:1–3)

It is hard to comprehend why Christians suffer the same problems as those who turn their backs on God. We get sick, injured, robbed, and so much worse. We aren't spared from harm and disease. But we do have one blessing not afforded to those outside the faith—the presence of the Lord to soothe and comfort us with peace and strength.

I have told you all this so that you may have peace in me. Here on earth you will have many trials and sorrows. But take heart, because I have overcome the world. (John 16:33)

Some people bring unnecessary suffering upon themselves due to their poor choices. Making godly choices does spare some believers from some problems—they are less likely to be afflicted by certain diseases, for example. But no life is left untouched at some point. Because the world we live in is in a state of decay, none of us are immune from suffering.

Job was attacked physically to test his loyalty and faith in the Lord. Satan hoped Job would blame God and turn away from him. It's quite possible the same happens today. Some of our afflictions happen, because spiritual warfare is at work, trying to get us to turn away from our faith in the Lord and our desire to become more like him.

Our fallen world's standard operating practice is due to the consequences of Adam and Eve's rebellion against God. For the most part, God does not veer from that, but occasionally he intervenes. He still performs miracles. Miracles go against the science of decay and destruction and make something new again—reverse sick cells and create health where there once was disease.

All Christ followers have received a spiritual miracle—God makes us new through the price Jesus paid on the cross. But some believers also receive physical miracles. Other times, God withholds the opportunity for a miracle so something even more significant can transpire. It's hard for us to fathom *why* with our finite minds. Truly the statement "God's ways are not our ways" is fitting. Souls matter more to God than physical wellness. Our physical status is temporary, but our spiritual wellbeing is for eternity.

Suffering Brings Opportunities

- **Conform to the example of Christ.** *[For my determined purpose is] that I may know Him [that I may progressively become more deeply and intimately acquainted with Him, perceiving and recognizing and understanding the wonders of His Person more strongly and more clearly], and that I may in that same way come to know the power outflowing from His resurrection [which it exerts over believers], and that I may so share His sufferings as to be continually transformed [in spirit into His likeness even] to His death, [in the hope] That if possible I may attain to the [spiritual and moral] resurrection [that lifts me] out from among the dead [even while in the body]* (Philippians 3:10–11 AMPC).

  For even to this were you called [it is inseparable from your vocation]. For Christ also suffered for you, leaving you [His personal] example, so that you should follow in His footsteps (1 Peter 2:21 AMPC).

- **Learn to trust in him and not in yourself.** *So we do not lose heart. Though our outer self is wasting away, our inner self is being renewed day by day* (2 Corinthians 4:16 ESV).

- **Wait for God's heavenly glory.** *For I consider that the sufferings of this present time are not worth comparing with the glory that is to be revealed to us* (Romans 8:18 ESV).

- **Develop maturity.** *And after you have suffered a little while, the God of all grace, who has called you to his eternal glory in*

Christ, will himself restore, confirm, strengthen, and establish you (1 Peter 5:10 ESV).

- **Gain endurance as you rejoice.** *Not only that, but we rejoice in our sufferings, knowing that suffering produces endurance* (Romans 5:3 ESV).

- **Tap in to God's grace, enough for whatever you lack.** *But he said to me, "My grace is sufficient for you, for my power is made perfect in weakness." Therefore I will boast all the more gladly of my weaknesses, so that the power of Christ may rest upon me* (2 Corinthians 12:9 ESV).

Family Recipes

Did you know that one in three people in the U.S. has a chronic illness? And there are 100 million Americans who live daily with chronic pain. It's essential to grasp what the Bible says about suffering, so we can cope when we are afflicted, and so we can minister to others who endure ongoing health problems.

Ingredients to Deal with Suffering

1. **Fill your day wisely, so you don't overdo it.** Limit your activities. Pray about what God wants you to do and what should be left undone. Just because you do less than before or choose different projects, doesn't make you less of a person.

2. **Take care of yourself, so you can be there for others.** If you allow yourself to get depleted, there's no energy or health left to be a blessing to others around you.

3. **Do what you can to relieve suffering in others and yourself.** This includes visiting orphans and widows (James 1:27) and sharing your resources with those in need (1 Timothy 6:18).

4. **Reduce fear and plug in to God's power, love, and ability to have a sound mind.** The basic needs of humanity involve

these elements, and fear is what interferes with our ability to find what we need (2 Timothy 1:7).

To Ponder

- Do I feel overwhelmed when I try to juggle my health problems and other life trials?

- Do I feel like I have it worse than others?

- Do I blame God for my suffering?

- Do I sense God's presence and grace when I'm in pain or ill?

- Am I willing to support someone else going through a difficult time, or am I buried in my own trials?

- Do I tend to overdo it and then get frustrated by my increased symptoms?

Instructions for Living

1. **Put others at ease.** Do your best to make them not feel uncomfortable about the fact that you are suffering from a chronic illness.

2. **Be more sympathetic to others who are suffering.** While relating to others, avoid comparing your problems to theirs—it makes them feel like you are one-upping their situations.

3. **Help others—this is often the best medicine!** Change the focus from inward to outward. Put a positive spin on being sick, so you take an active role rather than a passive one. You are no longer a victim, but a survivor or overcomer.

4. **Pray with others in need.** If you've ever suffered from chronic symptoms, you know how meaningful it is to have someone pray with you. Prayer is a major tool for supporting a person who is ill or disabled.

Questions

Read the testimony of Asaph in Psalm 73:1–28.

1. Asaph was upset about a certain unfairness in life. What was it?

2. Read verses 1–15. What verse do you most relate to when you are in a "woe is me" mood?

3. Read verses 16–20, 27. What eventually happens to those who aren't part of God's family? Do they continue to prosper and not face suffering?

4. Read verses 21–28. Like Asaph, list your shortcomings. Next, find all the reasons you can praise God even when you are suffering, based on these verses.

The passage ends with a promise to tell others of God's goodness. How can you, in the midst of your suffering, find the right words (and mean them) to tell others about the wonderful works of God?

Family Legacy

Is God leading you to consider ministering to those who are chronically ill—either in your family or in your community? Part of your legacy is using your time and energy to help those who aren't able to manage as well.

Attitudes to Consider

- Just because they look okay and act okay, doesn't mean they feel okay. Many try to look as normal as possible on the outside. If you care, you must learn to read them for signs of suffering. Ask them sincerely how they are doing—and truly listen!

- Someone robbed of good health is going through the same stages of grief as when they lose someone they love. Identify their stage of grief and minister to it. (1) Shock and denial,

(2) pain and guilt, (3) anger and bargaining, (4) depression, reflection or loneliness, (5) the upward turn, (6) reconstruction, and (7) acceptance and hope.

- You don't know or understand anything, unless you've gone through it yourself. Don't say, "I understand" to someone who is suffering. It might cause them to put up a protective barrier to additional comments, because they feel like you couldn't possibly understand. Don't tell them it's just like when you had the flu, or when you had a baby, or when you were up sick all night. Having chronic disease or pain is nothing at all like a temporary discomfort. It is a life sentence of suffering.

- When they are suffering silently, pray about how you can help them. When they overdo it, give them permission to say "no," but don't preach at them for overdoing it. Also, don't pile on more guilt by insisting they be more involved in something, "because they'll feel better if they get their minds off their problems."

- Acknowledge their struggle without telling them they need to be brave. Ask, "I can see this is a heavy burden for you. How may I pray for you?"

- Don't feel compelled to share every cure you hear about with them. They have heard all sorts of remedies and have determined their own course of treatment. When you press them to try certain remedies, they feel like you are trying to fix them, and they don't want to be your project. They don't want to feel like they've failed by not responding to treatment. They already experience the burden of spending money on concoctions that didn't work. They've researched every option they can find. They know their situation better than you do. Instead of "fixing" them, they need you to be their refuge from this sort of pressure.

- If you are close to someone who isn't savvy when it comes to medical research, you can offer to be their advocate and researcher, but make sure they still feel like they are the one calling the shots.

Be Flexible to Their Needs

- Keep in mind, the ill person already feels like a burden. This burden could be financial, physical, emotional, spiritual, or a mixture of all. It sometimes leads to frustration and hopelessness. The sufferer might withdraw as a way to cope.

- Realize that the individual could be suffering from physical discomfort or downright pain. Sometimes they are agitated and can't keep still. They seldom get enough sleep. Thoughts race, and they can't slow down their minds.

- Know when to stay away or move closer.

- Sit and listen without judgment or comment.

- Speak with hope to them, while remaining honest and realistic as you encourage them.

- Be understanding when fatigue or other symptoms causes a friend to cancel plans at the last minute. Continue to include her in your future plans.

Losing Friends Due to Disability

There are only two types of people reading this chapter: those who are disabled with chronic health conditions and those who are healthy but have a disabled friend or loved one. There really isn't another category. And often, we are both!

One of the hardest experiences for someone who suffers from symptoms and side effects isn't the health conditions or the treatments—it's the relationships that suffer. One of my closest friends, Shelly*, said she couldn't handle how much my health got in the way of our friendship, and so she wrote me a note basically breaking up with me. She didn't have the mental energy needed to be strong, even though I told her she didn't have to be strong for me.

> The main ingredient for helping someone is simply showing up.

I just wanted her to be available for support. But she said even that was too hard. Shelly wanted a friend that could be and do the things she wanted in a friendship. And she admitted it didn't matter that I was there for her hard stuff. She was done and wanted out. I wasn't to contact her—she would contact me when she wanted. She declared that the friendship would be on her terms.

Of course, as I'm writing this I see all over again how this wasn't the kind of relationship we *thought* we had. We expected to remain close no matter what we were going through for the good or for the bad. Then she asked for a friendship divorce. (Since then she is back to being a periphery friend, and neither of us has bitterness. I mourn what we lost, and I'm guessing she does too.)

The timing hit when I really needed a friend. I'd invested what energy I had into being a friend to her, and I hadn't developed other close friendships. Suddenly, besides having many casual acquaintances, I didn't have anyone other than my husband. He is a great friend, but let's face it, we should never expect our spouses to meet every single need we have. That's too much to put on any one individual.

I had to learn a new way of building friendships. I discovered it was best to disclose my health issues when moving from acquaintance to friend status. I'm honest regarding what I can bring to the table as a friend—as well as what I need in a friend.

Practical Ways to Help

- Offer to drive them places or arrange rides for them. Even if they can drive, this conserves energy, so they can enjoy the activity more.

- Arrange for meals not merely during acute times of need such as after birth, death, or surgery, but also when they suffer flares in chronic symptoms and are unable to prepare meals for themselves.

- Cards, phone calls, and visits are nice at the hospital and also at home. Don't wait for crisis situations to help. And remember, cards that say "I'm thinking of you" or "I'm praying for you" might be more appropriate than a get-well card.

- People are at a loss of what to say. Just because you're not sure exactly what to say, by all means—say something! This is not the time to avoid someone because of your own uncertainties. You will hurt to see your friend in pain. But it's okay to talk out these feelings with your friend rather than avoiding them. The main ingredient for helping someone is simply showing up.

- You don't always have to talk. In fact, when someone is feeling poorly, it is often difficult for them to work at listening. Ask them if they feel like making conversation, or if they just want you to be there. See if it's okay for you to pray aloud for them. Give them permission to rest. Bring a book, so they don't feel they must entertain you.

- Be sincere when you ask, "How do you feel today?" Breathe, and give them a chance to say how they really feel. After asking about their health, don't tell them how good they look. They just told you how awful they feel! They need their symptoms and feelings validated.

- Research their illness, and become familiar with their symptoms and their treatments.

Specific Ways to Help

- Be detailed in your offer to help. Name a task or chore, and give them a couple of options for when you can assist them with the project. Ask them if they would mind if you help. Remember, if you vaguely offer to help, they probably won't take you up on it.

- Do your grocery shopping together. Offer for them to go along with you. Sometimes those with chronic conditions want to get out of the house, but they need assistance. Or, if they are homebound, take their lists, and do it for them. Another option is to order online and take them to pick up curbside. On the way there, go through a drive-thru to get a beverage to enjoy while waiting for delivery.

- Have a house cleaning party. This is especially helpful during the holidays or before visitors arrive.

- Run errands together, or offer to do them for her.

- Get your hair done together.

- Take them to doctor appointments. If they wish, sit with them in the exam room as a support system, to help sort out information and instructions the doctors may have. Offer to pick up prescription medications on the way home from the physician.

- Double your recipe for dinner, and deliver half to them.

- Join in a hobby they are still able to enjoy. Patients don't always want to focus on their illnesses and would love to occupy their time doing things that make them feel useful or relaxed.

- Offer to do laundry, yardwork, babysitting, or other chores and errands.

- Write a letter of encouragement to them. Write thank-you notes for them. Help with any other correspondence they may have.

- Offer to play games or read to help pass the time.

- Send flowers, balloons, reading materials, and other small gifts appropriate to their needs.

- If you have the means, help financially if there is a need.

Avoid Theses Savior Phrases

- God doesn't give you more than you can handle.

- We all have our crosses to bear.

- I know just how you feel.

- Don't worry. Let go and let God.

- All things work together for good. Cheer up.

- God is using this to refine you.

- If you had more faith you would be healed. There must be sin in your life.

- Don't claim it and you won't have it.

- I bet you'd feel a hundred times better if you lost some of that weight.

- Just don't dwell on it. Think about positive things, and you'll feel better.

- You just need more (insert exercise, positive attitude, essential oil, natural remedy, etc.)

- By his stripes you are healed.

Why not?

I posted a survey on Facebook and asked others who deal with chronic conditions to share the phrases they are told that hurt their hearts. The above list contains just a few of the many responses I received. It was obvious I had hit a nerve. But I also received this question from a responder, "So, what are you ladies looking for besides a listening ear . . . or, is that *all* you want? I have a 'chronic' illness so I can understand some of this, but other comments from this list I feel are helpful or encouraging."

Why are savior phrases not helpful? Because it puts the one suffering in a position of feeling like they are being attacked or misunderstood. A Christ follower can fully believe the content of a Bible passage but still not feel encouraged when it is quoted *at* them rather than *for* them.

> Suffering qualifies us to join the club with Jesus.

Some believe that the devil only knows what we are fighting if we say it aloud, so they think admitting suffering is a way to invite a spiritual attack. I'm not sure where they find that in Scripture. They also believe whatever label we proclaim (like a diagnosis) is causing it to be true in our lives, so they recommend not saying anything we don't want in our lives. We aren't that powerful, people! But God is, and he wants to hear our hearts, holding nothing back.

Our accusers don't know what to do when something chronic hits their own lives. It seems the same trial that was meant as punishment in our lives was given to them *because* of their faithfulness. They say they must be doing something right for trouble to come visit them. How can we have it both ways? The fact is, it rains on the just and the unjust (see Matthew 5:45).

By revealing these savior phrases, I'm offering a new kind of sensitivity training. I want to reveal how hurtful these are to people who are already hurting enough. Sometimes the intent is pure, but misguided or uninformed. And sometimes the motive is exactly as it seems, to make the one who isn't suffering look superior to the one who is enduring great hardship. The best approach is to seek discernment from God before speaking to someone who is hurting and ask God to guide your words.

> Suffering does not automatically qualify us to grow in the Lord. It merely gives us the opportunity to grow or to groan.

Some will welcome suggestions, while others have researched and tried everything—they simply need prayers.

On one thing I want to be very clear. As "The Grin Gal" I know it's possible to experience joy *and* sadness at the same time. Or joy *and* [fill-in-the-blank]. Faking anything (faith, joy, you name it) doesn't honor the suffering. Here is some good news though. Suffering qualifies us to join the club with Jesus. We enter into the fellowship of the suffering of Christ. This shows a couple of concepts. (1) Suffering isn't a sin problem, or Jesus would have been a sinner when he suffered. (2) Suffering somehow allows us to partner and participate with Christ. I'll sign up for that any day, no matter the cost.

> *That I may know Him and the power of His resurrection, and the fellowship of His sufferings, being conformed to His death.* (Philippians 3:10 NKJV)

Family Chat

During the focus group session, Hally Wells reassured us that God gives us the words to say to others going through tough times, even when we are in the midst of our own trials. She reminded us that this happens as long as we seek his direction in what we say and do, and as long as we continue to have a spirit of gratitude even though we have crummy circumstances. This will color our attitudes regarding our own suffering and allow us to encourage others in the midst of their suffering. Hally pointed out that all sorts of loss, not just physical loss, gives us an opportunity to grow spiritually and to strengthen our faith.

Suffering does not automatically qualify us to grow in the Lord. It merely gives us the opportunity to grow or to groan. If we choose to allow it to shape us into his image, then it's a prime time for spiritual maturity.

Closing Prayer

Father, I bring you all the physical suffering around me and in me. All the pain and symptoms my loved ones deal with on a regular basis. Chronic anything is just plain awful! I yield it to you for you to bring glory to yourself and to expand your kingdom. Help me not wallow in my trials and symptoms but find a way to rejoice that I join Jesus in the fellowship of his suffering. And help me be alert to the opportunities you give me, so I shine the light on you when others are hurting. Amen.

Chapter Seven

WHEN I'M DESTITUTE

Satan wiped out all of Job's possessions and material goods. He had to start from scratch. If you've ever lost a job, a home, or had a financial reversal, you know the challenge of starting over. What words of comfort and strength can you find from Scripture to help you hold on to hope? This chapter will help you when you feel destitute and equip you to encourage others as they face similar challenges.

Family Album

The Transformation of Fresh Starts

God loves to transform his children from wooden marionettes to real live boys and girls. We are his Pinocchio stories. Most of us remember the childhood tale. Geppetto the wood carver wishes upon a star that Pinocchio might come to life. Children still wish upon a star with the words "Star light, star bright, first star I see tonight, I wish I may, I wish I might, have the wish I wish tonight."

The good news is, God has the power to transform. Rather than making wishes, we can pray to our Creator, and he enjoys re-creating us in his image. When we deal with financial blows, it is a perfect opportunity for transformation. We will change, or our situation will change—either way God will be present and at work! Consider the symbolism in the story of Pinocchio.

> God loves to transform his children from wooden marionettes to real live boys and girls.

We are Pinocchio. The strings represent the things we allow to motivate us, control us, and even send us on guilt trips. The wood represents our limitations. And the puppet-like jerky motions are our best intentions, almost God-like, but missing the Breath of Life when we try to do it on our own.

In the story, even after the Blue Fairy touches Pinocchio with her magic wand, he goes through a transformation process—a challenge. Pinocchio must make wise choices and prove himself to be brave, truthful, and unselfish. He is instructed, "Be a good boy and always let your conscience be your guide."

In the life of believers, the Holy Spirit is our guide. Our attitudes and actions reflect whether we are following his direction or still trying to do life in our own strength. When we are destitute, there is no way we can handle situations on our own. Transformation happens when we realize the Holy Spirit, our Inner Mentor, illuminates the truth.

Pinocchio is tested before he earns the right to be a real boy. We are tested after we are adopted into God's family. These testings and trials help grow us, shape us, mold us. Just like Geppetto chiseled wood to shape a marionette and then sanded away the rough edges, God fashions us into the creation he wants us to be.

Probably the most famous part of the story is when Pinocchio gets caught telling lie after lie to cover his antics. The Blue Fairy designed his nose to grow longer every time he told a lie.

God transforms us through truth. His truth—found in his Word. Pinocchio is given a buddy named Jiminy Cricket, designed to be Pinocchio's conscience. There are two problems: first, Pinocchio chooses *not* to listen to Jiminy when something more adventurous comes his way, and secondly, Jiminy's foibles keep him from being a perfect conscience. We do have perfect discernment through Scripture and the Holy Spirit. Yet, like Pinocchio we often make choices during the transformation process that cause us to slow down God's work in us.

Pinocchio skips school to go off with the crafty fox, Honest John. What a perfect symbol of the devil, intent on misleading us. When Pinocchio buys in to the fox's lie, he gets sold to Stromboli, the gypsy caravan man. Pinocchio becomes the star of the marionette show as the puppet without strings. Yet he realizes that sort of success has a great cost—he misses his father, Geppetto. Stromboli imprisons Pinocchio in a cage and takes him to the next town on the tour.

> Perhaps in the losing, we actually end up gaining—transformed and renewed.

How often do we miss out on fellowship with our heavenly Father when we go traipsing after Satan's deception in search of success? When we lose our jobs, our possessions, our homes, we are tempted to find quick-fix solutions. But are they based on God's direction or "Honest John"?

The Blue Fairy rescues Pinocchio out of his cage, and Pinocchio spins another tale about why he's not in school. His nose grows and grows. Shamed by the mess he's gotten himself into, Pinocchio begs for mercy.

Our heavenly Father rescues us out of all our messes and gives us almost limitless second chances. The act of transformation often has lots of starts and stops and do-overs. Mercy indeed.

In the end, the Blue Fairy frees Pinocchio, shrinks his nose, and sends him home to Geppetto.

Sometimes it's the journey that causes us to learn the lessons that transform us most. Just as Pinocchio lived out his days as Geppetto's real live boy, we get to enjoy being our Creator's children.

In this chapter, as we see what it's like to endure material loss, keep in mind that there's always an opportunity for a do-over—a fresh start. Perhaps in the losing, we actually end up gaining—transformed and renewed.

Family Bible

Job lost so much in such a short time. Can you imagine the sense of floundering he must have experienced, trying to get his business back up and running after it essentially crashed? This, while not only experiencing the grief of losing all his children in one fell swoop but also enduring the attacks of serious health issues. And his support system consisted of friends, family, and spiritual advisers who were not empathetic or even theologically accurate.

> *All praise to God, the Father of our Lord Jesus Christ. It is by his great mercy that we have been born again, because God raised Jesus Christ from the dead. Now we live with great expectation, and we have a priceless inheritance—an inheritance that is kept in heaven for you, pure and undefiled, beyond the reach of change and decay. And through your faith, God is protecting you by his power until you receive this salvation, which is ready to be revealed on the last day for all to see.*
>
> *So be truly glad. There is wonderful joy ahead, even though you must endure many trials for a little while. These trials*

will show that your faith is genuine. It is being tested as fire tests and purifies gold—though your faith is far more precious than mere gold. So when your faith remains strong through many trials, it will bring you much praise and glory and honor on the day when Jesus Christ is revealed to the whole world.

You love him even though you have never seen him. Though you do not see him now, you trust him; and you rejoice with a glorious, inexpressible joy. The reward for trusting him will be the salvation of your souls. (1 Peter 1:3–9)

Peter addressed how we feel when we face loss and trials. He answers the questions we have and reminds us of the blessings we have in Christ. His point of view reminds me of the hymn by Esther K. Rusthoi, "It Will Be Worth It All When We See Jesus." When we feel dead from our loss, we have a certain hope of feeling alive again through the resurrection. One day, our physical resurrection will come, but in the meantime, we have spiritual renewal available that lifts us from the depths of our suffering.

The miracle of the resurrection has dominance over any trial, any loss. What we can't do on our own, we can experience, because we have an all-powerful God who is able. Easter isn't just a hunt for eggs and a sugar rush, it's an event we must keep in the forefront of our minds, all year round. It is the reminder that God can overcome any loss and bring something new from it. From ashes to beauty.

Peter reminded the readers of this passage that no trial can keep us from praising God for what he has done and will do. He assures us that trials refine us and mature us. He highlights the hope we have in Jesus—a hope that those outside the faith cannot experience as they suffer setbacks. Death and loss no longer have any control over us. They are temporary interruptions in the scheme of what matters. Loss of any kind is virtually an empty threat, because it's not permanent. It has no power to devastate and derail us—unless we let it. It's like our shadows trying to box us. No real danger!

Peter describes this hope we have as imperishable—it can't spoil, run out, or expire. We have an unending supply of hope. Because of this source of hope, Peter has the audacity to suggest we can actually rejoice in our suffering. I know what you're thinking—now we're taking it too far. How can anyone in their sound mind, if they are honest, feel like rejoicing (celebrating with joy) while going through terrible times? Peter acknowledges life isn't going to be flawless—"even though you must endure many trials for a little while."

> Loss of any kind is virtually an empty threat, because it's not permanent. It has no power to devastate and derail us—unless we let it.

When we don't allow the pain of temporary trials to render us ineffective in our relationship with the Lord and as a servant for his good purposes, God is able to produce miracles that draw others to him. In the end, he is glorified more. Faith doesn't eradicate pain, but it does introduce hope. It's not that Peter is suggesting we don't experience the torment of pain during times of loss. No way. To do so would minimize the pain Jesus experienced too.

No matter the severity of the pain, it does not have to defeat us. God has every resource we need to live a victorious life even before we get to the other side of our trials. This lesson Job learned in the Old Testament, and the lesson Peter taught others in the New Testament, is the same one we can aspire to live out today.

Faith in a resurrected Savior means a new way of viewing and doing life. What we see with our physical eyes isn't all there is to life. We have so much more! Yes, we experience loss, but that is a surface issue. The deeper issue is how close or far away do we feel from God during our suffering and grief? God stocked up enough hope and joy in his shelter for every emergency. Bombs of life could be going off, tornado-trials swirling around, but we are safe and secure in his refuge.

When we are severely tested, there might be times we are tempted to say we have no use for God—to question where he is in our time of need. We feel neglected, rejected. Abandoned. When that happens, we need to dive in to Scripture. The Word of God is alive, active, and powerful. It can speak to our inner beings in a way that makes sense—enough to shoo away the emotions of defeat and despair with a reassurance that God's promise is reliable and true.

> *Through him we have also obtained access by faith into this grace in which we stand, and we rejoice in hope of the glory of God. Not only that, but we rejoice in our sufferings, knowing that suffering produces endurance, and endurance produces character, and character produces hope, and hope does not put us to shame, because God's love has been poured into our hearts through the Holy Spirit who has been given to us.* (Romans 5:2–5 ESV)

Look at the building blocks of the faith here. Our access key is faith, and it unlocks our entry to grace. Because of God's glory, and our hope in him, we can rejoice. Not just being happy during the good times, though—we are able to celebrate God during our trials. We can rejoice when we go through terrible trials, because we know that's when we grow up in our faith. Our Christian growth chart includes the following steps, according to Romans 5:2–5:

- Faith as our foundation
- Suffering
- Endurance
- Character
- Hope

Looking at this in reverse, the way to find the hope to which we cling is to have strong character. Strength of character comes from having the ability to endure suffering. Endurance is built when we can put up with anything that tries to hold us back. We move forward despite being pulled down through our trials and suffering.

> *Therefore I tell you, do not be anxious about your life, what you will eat or what you will drink, nor about your body, what you will put on. Is not life more than food, and the body more than clothing? Look at the birds of the air: they neither sow nor reap nor gather into barns, and yet your heavenly Father feeds them. Are you not of more value than they? And which of you by being anxious can add a single hour to his span of life?*

> *And why are you anxious about clothing? Consider the lilies of the field, how they grow: they neither toil nor spin, yet I tell you, even Solomon in all his glory was not arrayed like one of these. But if God so clothes the grass of the field, which today is alive and tomorrow is thrown into the oven, will he not much more clothe you, O you of little faith? Therefore do not be anxious, saying, "What shall we eat?" or "What shall we drink?" or "What shall we wear?" For the Gentiles seek after all these things, and your heavenly Father knows that you need them all.*

> *But seek first the kingdom of God and his righteousness, and all these things will be added to you. Therefore do not be anxious about tomorrow, for tomorrow will be anxious for itself. Sufficient for the day is its own trouble.* (Matthew 6:25–34 ESV)

We often put more priority in material possessions than we should, and when we lose them, it devastates us. Events that could draw us closer to God only serve to separate us if we are more concerned with what we've lost than what we have in Jesus Christ. Counselors recommend we hold on to our things loosely rather than having a tight grip on them. That way, when we lose what we never really owned in the first place, we'll rest in a contentment we never could have experienced if we felt like we deserved those material possessions.

Even as I'm preparing this manuscript to send to the editor, I have had another personal setback. We hope to move closer to where Russ works, so we put our home on the market. It went into contract—celebrations! After much difficulty finding a home in the new location that would work for our needs, we placed a contingent contract on the new house. We spent money on various inspections and contract options. We started packing to move. Then bad news hit—our buyer backed out. More bad news—the seller dissolved our contingency offer on our new place. We never outgrow the disappointment of loss, do we?

It's all a matter of stewardship—realizing God owns it all, and sometimes he lends part of it to us to use to expand his Kingdom—and even to bring us happiness. We are to take care of it, respect it, but not idolize it or covet what someone else has. Once we get the stewardship principles figured out, it helps as we process loss.

Family Recipes

No one wants to be an expert on the subject of loss. How many of us can raise our hands that we believe we've experienced more than our fair share of devastation? What is fair anyway? I've had to learn to ask, "Why *not* me?" rather than "Why me?" Read Paul's account of suffering in 2 Corinthians 11:16–33. If you were to write your story of loss in a similar style, what would it include? Here's mine:

- As a child, I grew up learning about **"elephants in the room"** like anger mismanagement, adultery, suicide, alcoholism, abuse, and bullies.

- I found out I was **barren** before I married. When engaged, my fiancé's friends suggested he dump me to find a wife who could bear his family. Russ ignored their helpfulness.

- My **father died** when I was only twenty-four.

- My boss's wife **falsely accused** me of having an affair with her husband. We prayed together as a staff each morning, that we would minister to the patients. Her accusations snuck up on me.

- **Chronic disease** disabled me at age twenty-eight. I traded dumbbells and workouts for medicine and naps.

- I **lost** some of my **support system** due to their false assumptions about my life situations. Either it wearied them, or they were skeptical of my symptoms, or they deemed the problems God's way of getting my attention, so I would "get right" with him.

- We dealt with **persecution** *by* the church (not *of* the church) as we served in full-time leadership in eleven churches. One church voted us out because we smiled too much, and I sat up too straight.

- We understood the word **"transplant"** a lot better than the word "rooted" with a total of twenty-eight addresses in our thirty-nine years of marriage, spread out over seventeen cities in six states.

- I have had **over 150** physicians, over 150 medications (not at the same time!), over 150 different tests, and 20+ surgeries.

- Rounds of **physical therapy** in twenty of the past thirty years, not to mention canes and wheelchairs.

- My former employer (and fellow church member) filed a **lawsuit**. I won, but at what cost?

- **Hurricanes** and **tornados** and **moving trucks**, oh my!

- Medical bills plus unemployment plus a lawsuit equaled **financial devastation**. During one economic reversal, we gave up the place where many of our life memories were made: a 4,000-square-foot home plus a two-story brick carriage house. We've also experienced the humiliation of food stamps and public assistance (and were grateful for them!).

What is your story of loss? Did you stay paralyzed by your loss, not sure how to process the stages of grief? Or did you find a way to move forward through God's direction? Please note it's only healthy to list your problems as a testimony of "our God is greater" than whatever *this* might be. It is not healthy to hit the *rewind* button over and over as you ruminate over the losses and wallow in pity.

> If you have suffered even one loss, you are qualified to tell others that God is enough.

If you have suffered even one loss, you are qualified to tell others that God is enough. His power is enough to overcome any circumstance—his peace is enough for you to endure any trial. Paul listed his trials as his resume. Job had a resume of suffering too. And few humans make it through life without their own list of losses. It's what we *do* with those losses that determines our outcome.

God's ways are not our ways. He loves to use the opposite of this world's values to show his power. When we are weak, then he is strong. And that's okay with me.

Ingredients to Peace While Destitute

1. **Trust in God to supply your needs.** *And my God will supply every need of yours according to his riches in glory in Christ Jesus* (Philippians 4:19 ESV).

2. **Focus on what you have, rather than what you lost.** *For we know that if the tent that is our earthly home is destroyed, we have a building from God, a house not made with hands, eternal in the heavens* (2 Corinthians 5:1 ESV).

3. **Sink into God's Word—the one true constant in your life.** *Heaven and earth will pass away, but my words will not pass away* (Matthew 24:35 ESV).

4. **Exchange fear for God's comfort.** *Even though I walk through the valley of the shadow of death, I will fear no evil, for you are with me; your rod and your staff, they comfort me* (Psalm 23:4 ESV).

5. **Ask God to give you his peace—a peace that will exceed all expectations.** *And the peace of God, which surpasses all understanding, will guard your hearts and your minds in Christ Jesus* (Philippians 4:7 ESV).

To Ponder

- What is this loss doing to me, emotionally and mentally?

- How do I feel about God right now? What do I know about God that can help me overcome any unbiblical feelings about him?

- How do I feel about my life right now? What do I know about my life that can help me overcome any unhealthy feelings about what might be ahead?

- What is the *one thing* I can do next to help me step out of the pit of misery?

Instructions for Living

1. **Recount the times God has delivered you from previous trials.** Remind yourself of the answered prayers, the blessings, and the provisions of previous hard times. We all go through

terrible circumstances, but don't forget the Lord sends help in a variety of ways. *Many are the afflictions of the righteous, but the LORD delivers him out of them all* (Psalm 34:19 ESV).

2. **Evaluate your priorities regarding material possessions.** *But seek first the kingdom of God and his righteousness, and all these things will be added to you* (Matthew 6:33 ESV).

3. **Value heavenly treasures more than earthly ones.** *Do not lay up for yourselves treasures on earth, where moth and rust destroy and where thieves break in and steal, but lay up for yourselves treasures in heaven, where neither moth nor rust destroys and where thieves do not break in and steal. For where your treasure is, there your heart will be also* (Matthew 6:19–21 ESV).

4. **Realize God entrusts resources to us, not only so we can exist, but also so we can show his love by helping others in need.** *But if anyone has the world's goods and sees his brother in need, yet closes his heart against him, how does God's love abide in him?* (1 John 3:17 ESV).

5. **Resist the urge to worry about your lack or loss of provisions.** *And which of you by being anxious can add a single hour to his span of life? And why are you anxious about clothing? Consider the lilies of the field, how they grow: they neither toil nor spin, yet I tell you, even Solomon in all his glory was not arrayed like one of these* (Matthew 6:27–29 ESV).

Questions

*   Can you think of a belonging that was damaged or lost that caused your heart to hurt? Why did it bother you so much? How did you get past it?

*   Is it wrong to enjoy the blessings of material possessions? At what point is a love of "things" inappropriate for Christ followers?

- Have you ever found your reactions about belongings to be out of balance? How did you readjust?

- If you had to start over because of a financial reversal or loss of home or job—how did it go? If you could do anything over, what would you do differently?

Family Legacy

When you're helping someone else through a time of loss (death, material goods, job, marriage, etc.) be mindful of these pointers:

What *Not* to Do

1. **Ask questions you already know the answer to.** Avoid asking how they are holding up, because they will feel like they have to put on a brave front.

2. **Ask "Is there anything I can do?"** Sufferers don't want to have to suggest ways you can help. They know they need help, but they are often too overwhelmed to even know how to inventory their needs. Instead of asking, offer to do a specific task or provide a specific need. Ask God to show you what your part in providing during this time of loss might look like.

3. **Empathize by saying, "The same thing happened to me. I know how you feel."** No two people on the planet process loss in the same way, and even if we did, the sufferer will feel like you are putting yourself in the spotlight rather than in their shoes. They don't want to think about your loss right then, because frankly, they are too absorbed by their own pain to think of much else. They are in survival mode.

4. **Minimize their loss to try to make them feel better.** Don't make comments such as: "At least you don't have it as bad as so-and-so." "Good thing you don't have kids at home as you go through this." "You can bounce back from this."

5. **Give remedies for their next steps.** Avoid swooping in to rescue them. We feel better when we're fixing things, but sometimes that's not our job. We don't get to wear the superhero cape. They might not be ready for tips on how to move on with life yet, and by you suggesting they add more normal routine to their day, they will feel more of a failure when they don't have the mental or physical energy to accomplish that yet.

6. **Say "Get back up on the horse."** Don't advise them to try for a new job, if they've lost theirs. They know that already. When we make suggestions of how to start over, we make it sound much simpler than it really is. And if they've lost a child to miscarriage, telling them "at least you can try again" is little comfort. Often, we want them to get back to our version of normal so we don't feel so terrible for experiencing normal while they're experiencing loss.

7. **Say "Time heals all wounds."** Reminding the sufferer things will be better—to just give it time—is not a comfort. Right now it likely feels like time is standing still.

What to Do

1. **Follow their lead.** If they are quiet, be quiet with them. If they want to talk, listen. If they ask your opinion, give short answers. Conversation should be a dance, and the grieving dance partner gets to lead.

2. **Acknowledge their loss.** It doesn't spare them more pain by avoiding a mention of their loss, but it validates their pain when you bring it up.

1. **Allow them to experience and express emotion.** We often downplay emotion, but it's an essential part of grief for any loss.

2. **Be patient with their behavior and responses.** They might

not be quite themselves for a while. Show love by tolerating any slip-ups they might have from the fog of their loss.

3. **Realize some losses take longer than others to process.** Give the gift of time. Use that period to show more support, more love, more understanding—than during normal times. Grace their grief.

4. **Notice what they are neglecting, and help fill in.** Some forget to eat—so don't just make a meal to drop off—offer to share a mealtime with them. Some are overwhelmed by the stack of bills. If you are in a close relationship with them, they might be open to your assistance. Loss causes people to feel like it takes twice as long to get half as much accomplished, so giving them relief from overwhelming to-do lists is a big help. They can expend the energy they've saved into healing from the loss.

Family Chat

When it seems like we've lost it all, it's important to remind ourselves that God never leaves or forsakes us. The rest can be rebuilt, or we can do without. Isn't it so human of us, when we lose something, to feel like we've lost it all—when in fact we still have what really matters—nothing will separate us from God!

> Conversation should be a dance, and the grieving dance partner gets to lead.

Luanne Lopez from focus group mentioned what it is like to lose it all, but also that it is okay to enjoy what God blesses us with. She said, "If God gave us the earth for our enjoyment, then we should enjoy the things we have that are earthly possessions. But he should always come first." Keeping that priority in mind is how we can manage both the loss and acquiring of things.

Robin Grunder also has experienced material loss. She explained that it's often the memories we made with the possession that makes us sad when we lose it—not materialism. It's okay to be sad. But let's also be grateful for the opportunity we had to make those memories in the first place! Memories mean we've shared love with others.

I pray God puts reminders in our paths to focus on him and on what he would have us learn through each trial we face. May we be a testimony of God's goodness even as we walk through the valleys of death and destitution. And when we have a hard time believing it, may God reinforce it in our own lives, so we can share our faith with authenticity.

Closing Prayer

Lord of my heart, I seek you to help in the way I deal with trials and how I help others going through them. Most of all, help me not lose sight of you when a trial tries to cloud my view of you. I pray for others hurting—that you will comfort them and strengthen them when it comes to the trials they are facing right now. Equip them for what is ahead, and use them in such amazing ways I can only point to you as the Orchestrator of our days. Amen.

CONCLUSION

If you've ever wondered if Job might be a member of your family tree . . . you might be right. You can certainly trace your lineage back to Noah, and perhaps Noah could trace his lineage back to Job—who knows? But even if we're not in his bloodline, we've inherited some of the same opportunities and challenges he faced.

Obviously, most of us will never be hit with the level of devastation that Satan used to tempt Job to fail. To act like our problems are "Job-like" is not meant to minimize what he went through. Our premise through the book has been that all humans suffer from loss. From studying how the Bible teaches us to handle these trials, we can come out praising God, just as Job ultimately did.

There's comfort in knowing someone before us has suffered the same trials we're experiencing. It's like all those saints come alongside of us, put their arms around us, and assure us that this current suffering won't last forever.

> We know the end of Job's story, but God is still writing our stories.

Satan believed Job's faithfulness was only because God had a hedge of protection around Job that kept him from being hit by any challenges that would cause him to curse God. God released that hedge to give Satan access to Job. Let us determine to pray for that hedge of protection, not just around us, but also around our loved ones. May God repel the fiery darts of Satan—that they bounce off us before they ever damage us.

We know the end of Job's story, but God is still writing our stories. How we choose to handle each life trial determines the ending of our tales. Now that we've studied the seven trials every woman faces, not only are we more equipped to deal with our own situations, we are better prepared to help others who endure suffering.

A Benediction for You

A compilation prayer inspired by Psalms 8, 17, and 20.

> May the LORD our God, the Majestic One, fill your life with his glory.
>
> May his strength silence your enemies and your own self-doubt.
>
> May the stars and moon point to the magnitude of his sovereignty. He is LORD.
>
> May he be your defense, your help in this time of need.
>
> May he pay attention to your transparent prayers as you plead your case.
>
> May you follow after his righteousness and examine your heart to reflect his.
>
> May your words and actions shadow his example and comply with his commands.
>
> May you avoid following those who do not follow after God. Do not seek their approval.
>
> May you keep your steps straight on his path and not stumble. (But when you do, he is merciful.)
>
> May God stoop down and listen to your prayers, and answer as he sees fit.
>
> May he show you his unfailing love—his wonderful ways.

May his mighty power rescue you and be your refuge.

May he hide you in the shadow of his wings.

May he protect you from your enemies—his enemies too.

May he stand against them and bring them to their knees!

May he satisfy your hunger—you are his treasured ones.

May your children have plenty, leaving an inheritance for their descendants.

May you pursue the LORD and be satisfied.

May the LORD answer your troubled cry.

May he keep you safe from all harm.

May he send you help from his sanctuary.

May he grant your heart's desires and make your God-led plans succeed.

May the LORD our God, the Majestic One, fill your life with his glory.

Amen.

It Starts Now!

As we close, don't forget our main Scripture concept. *No test or temptation that comes your way is beyond the course of what others have had to face. All you need to remember is that God will never let you down; he'll never let you be pushed past your limit; he'll always be there to help you come through it* (1 Corinthians 10:13 MSG).

Life is one big trial. But through it all we get to be witnesses—and leave it up to God to be the judge!

FAMILY HOPE CHEST

Not a Trite Platitude

When my focus group went through this book before publication, the members were going through deep waters, barely keeping their heads above water. I wrote this note to them, to encourage their hearts to endure the trials.

> I hate it when someone gives me a platitude that just makes me feel worse! So first off, I want to say that I'm with you—what you have been going through stinks! It hurts. It's not fair. It's not even bearable. And it hurts more, because it's so-called *people of God* hurting you the most. And in your position, it's hard to have a support system, because you probably feel very guarded in what you say about your situation to others. You must feel like you are about to crumble.

> One thing I've been learning through my own issues is that I can't get everything right, others can't get everything right, and it feels useless to try sometimes. God showed me the only thing I had to concentrate on was being close to him. And some of you are angry with God right now, so being in a close relationship with him is not as easy as it sounds. Some of you admit your anger stems from knowing God is in control and wondering why he is allowing these trials going on in your lives. With that question on your heart, it must be difficult to want to crawl up in Papa God's lap for any sort of intimacy. Without

that closeness in place, everything else looks and feels worse and situations snowball.

Is it extra hard when those around you seem so happy? When you're hurting, seeing others be happy emphasizes the gap between your downward frame of mind and the optimism and success of others. You probably can't imagine being content, in this "winter of your discontent" as one book describes a bad time.

When something doesn't happen that I want or like (or doesn't happen on my timetable), I remind myself that God's ways aren't my ways, and his time isn't my time. When I finally feel at peace trusting him even if it seems he's not my advocate, the change of outlook helps me cope. This ability to cope gives me hope even before the situation gets any better.

The trial you're in right now seems like it will never end, but it will. This is temporary! What a blessing to know we'll enjoy a timeless eternity after the suffering of this life is over. It will seem like such a short moment in comparison to the joy we will experience in eternity. It's sort of like the pain of childbirth. It lasts a while—and during it you might think you can't take it anymore. You need that baby out—*now!*

After the baby has come and you have that special moment of bonding, the memory of your childbirth pain pales in comparison to the joy of that relationship with this special little one. That's the best way I know to describe that our wait is going to be worth it. We're going to see this present suffering in a different light when we get to heaven. God knows how that is going to work out. As much as it pains him to see us hurting, he knows it ends. And he knows the good stuff yet to come. He has a different frame of reference than we have while we're going through trials, because he knows the rest of the story.

We all want Jesus to say "peace be still" to the storms in our lives and for everything that's wrong to be righted all at once. But more often than not, there's a rollercoaster of good and bad. Is there something you can think on differently, to help you fall in love with the Lord all over again (your first love)? Or in a fresh new way? There are no other relationships worth working to improve that matters as much as this one!

What can you lay down that you're still holding on to? Is there something you can ask God to release you from that makes you feel in bondage in some way? Do you need to walk away from something that is causing these wounds?

> **Where would we be without God's guidance? He's our compass when we lose the map!**

Have you considered consulting a counseling ministry for help processing the hurt? May the Lord remove one of the pressure points (or more!) so that you see a glimmer of hope.

When We've Lost the Map

We can praise God despite the trials.

- God holds my hand.
- God is my strength.
- God is more than enough.
- God is my refuge.
- God is my guide.

Where would we be without God's guidance? During hard times it seems we lose the map for a while and struggle with finding the way. Yet there's a peace that in him we won't *really* be lost. He's our compass when we lose the map! Besides, how can we really be lost when God is holding our hands? I love imagining that intimate scene.

Not only is he our source of strength, everything that makes him God is enough. *More* than enough. Plenty sufficient!

When we want to hide, he is our refuge. He gives us a place to feel safe and secure. When the world is against us, when we even attack ourselves through self-sabotage, there's one we can turn to who will kiss our boo-boos and reassure us that it really will be okay.

We don't need a map. God knows the way. He *is* the way. And with him, we are on our way to wherever he dwells.

Philippians 4:4-9, Personalized

I read Philippians 4:4–9 in several Bible versions and paraphrases. Then I personalized it. After speaking it for my own life, I read through this again as prayers for your life. As you do the same, we create a chain reaction. Let's encourage each other. We are in this together.

> I'm going to celebrate my God and rejoice in him. He is my delight. May these rejoicings echo in my heart and in yours. I pray I can encourage others to hold tight to the Lord. May they see my heart through my acts of kindness, and may I project an attitude of gentleness and patience. Not for my glory but to point to God. His presence is near!

> I'm choosing not to allow worry to rule my thoughts or feelings. Instead, I take what could be worry and shape them into prayers. God is big enough to handle it all, and I have no control anyway. So I trust in him. (Sometimes I have to remind myself of that!)

> As my mind makes a list of what I need, I turn it over to God. And as I think of the Lord's faithfulness, my concerns turn to praise. God is so good! He knows everything I think and feel even before I put my finger on what it is.

> Because of how good God is, he helps everything come together to a better good, even though that seems impossible in these challenging circumstances. Knowing that God has a handle on this helps to settle everything that feels so unsettled right now. This is why I can thank him even before the blessing arrives.

> When God kicks my worries to the curb, the vacancy left be-

hind is filled with his peace. He reassures me and explains that I don't need to understand it to believe it. May God's peace guard my heart and mind because of what Jesus has done on earth and in my life.

It is my best choice to fill my mind with God things. I will replace focusing on my messes with reflecting on all the good things. All that is true, honorable, reputable, righteous, pure, wholesome, lovely, gracious, admirable and brings peace.

I will think about what produces excellence (not what stirs up negative outcomes). I will focus on all the praiseworthy aspects of life instead of what's wrong with this world. I will be on the lookout for what is beautiful rather than what is despicable. I will put into practice what my spiritual mentors have taught me through Scripture and through their God-honoring lives. As I do that, the same God who helps all things work together for good will sing into me a beautiful harmony. He is the source of my peace and wellbeing, and he never leaves me. I will praise his name forever.

The Great Divide

Now, more than ever, I'm feeling the pressure of the great divide all around me. There are so many issues where people are taking sides. They either assume I'm on their side, or they judge me and assume I'm on the other side. They do this without even asking my view or my reasons!

> When God kicks my worries to the curb, the vacancy left behind is filled with his peace.

To be honest, I'm more of a "Why can't we all just get along?" kind of gal. I don't want there to be sides. We can be mature enough to respect people who have different viewpoints than us. Do we have to match in opinions to make relationships work? I would hope there's space for grace.

There are so many differing opinions these days:

- Masks or no masks?
- Self-isolating/social distancing or back to normal?
- Republican or Democrat?
- All Lives Matter or Black Lives Matter?
- Homeschooling or public education?
- Big churches, small churches, or home church?
- Technology-centric or simple-focus?

What do I do when people make a wrong assumption about me? Or worse, they judge me because of that assumption? What can *you* do?

Don't label fear in someone unless you know their brave story.

> *Love one another with brotherly affection [as members of one family], giving precedence and showing honor to one another.* (Romans 12:10 AMPC)

How to engage with grace, not disgrace:

1. Ask yourself if the battle is more important than the relationship.

2. Will the issue matter five years from now? If it's temporary, you can get past it.

3. Start conversations by acknowledging how you value the other person.

4. Tell your story rather than merely discussing facts. They can't argue with your life experience or debate it.

5. Resist stirring the pot by making divisive statements.

6. Ask them for permission to discuss it before bringing up subjects that divide.

7. Decide in advance what you will do if the conversation gets uncomfortable.

8. Don't drag others into the dispute. No one likes being put in the middle of someone else's battle.

9. Avoid making personal accusations to make your point. In debate we were taught you can tell when a side is losing when they start to attack the person rather than debate the issue.

> Don't label fear in someone unless you know their brave story.

10. Don't make it your life mission to change people's minds on things that don't matter for eternity.

Therefore I, a prisoner for serving the Lord, beg you to lead a life worthy of your calling, for you have been called by God. Always be humble and gentle. Be patient with each other, making allowance for each other's faults because of your love. Make every effort to keep yourselves united in the Spirit, binding yourselves together with peace. (Ephesians 4:1–3)

Some things I'm doing:

- I'm listening more and talking less.

- I'm evaluating why certain opinions matter so much to me that I'd be willing to hurt a relationship to be right. The answer is, nothing matters more to me than people.

- I ask Jesus to show me the hearts of others as he sees them. Usually he shows me they are hurting—not hurting me.

- I'm learning to appreciate diversity. Differences can be beautiful, like a garden filled with various flowers.

- I'm finding common ground rather than fixating on our differences.

Today what will you do to be part of the bridge and not part of the divide?

LEADER
DISCUSSION GUIDE

Note to Leaders: I am available to visit with your group either in person or online as you kick off or conclude this study.

Contact information:

kathy@kathycarltonwillis.com

956-642-6319 (text)

WEEK ONE: KICKOFF

Together, you will read over the introduction and use it as a guide for setting up the study for future weeks.

Mixer

Download signature card from www.kathycarltonwillis.com or create your own.

- **I've been doubted**
- **I've been disrespected**
- **I've been deserted**
- **I've been deceived**
- **I've been disappointed**
- **I've been disabled**
- **I've been destitute**

Instructions for the Mixer

If you have a large group, divide it into smaller groups. Within each small group encourage the women to interact. Ask the ladies to choose one of the trials they have dealt with and sign the lines on the signature card. They will probably be able to sign any of these lines, but the idea is to get the group talking about their previous trials in a way that isn't so serious or heavy. So have them pick one and move on to someone else in the group, so that it is a true social mixer.

If they aren't sure what some of these lines mean, here are more clues:

- **I've been doubted.** Have you had a friend second-guess you or question your words?

- **I've been disrespected.** Have you ever been accused or judged? Have words from others made you feel defensive?

- **I've been deserted.** Have you ever had someone walk out of your life when you needed them? Have you felt lonely or invisible?

- **I've been deceived.** Have you ever been taught or led by a spiritual leader in a way that manipulated Scripture to fit an agenda or to spiritually abuse you?

- **I've been disappointed.** Have you ever had unmet expectations from those you love most? Or they had unrealistic expectations of you?

- **I've been disabled.** Have you dealt with an illness, surgery, or injury that made you feel sidelined from life?

- **I've been destitute.** Have you ever lost a job or a home or dealt with reduced income?

Discussion Questions

- Do you have any sayings that help you cope when trials hit?
- What do you know about the story of Job in the Bible?

Navigate the Book

Point out the following sections so everyone understands the flow of the book. Each chapter is divided into the following segments to go along with the *Family Tree* theme:

- **Family Album**

  This section includes word snapshots of real-life stories—some serious, some humorous—all heart-warming. Not all are from my own life—but they come from my observations on life, whether I experienced it, witnessed it, or someone else shared it with me.

- **Family Bible**

  It's important to discuss how to overcome the trials we experience from a biblical perspective. I'm calling this section *Family Bible,* because I'm reminded how families have a family Bible they pass down from generation to generation. It records births, deaths, and often contains a pressed flower. But it also possesses the underlined Scriptures deemed important or inspirational by our ancestors.

- **Family Recipes**

  Families also pass along recipes from one generation to another. If we could pass anything on to our descendants, it would be the life lessons that will help them grow and experience success God's way. This section includes life application suggestions, or action steps, with discussion questions for personal discovery. Self-help books fail if they focus only on self, so this section provides practical steps from God's guidance to help you create a better life trial verdict.

- **Family Legacy**

  Living out our faith with other people is the final stage of the process. We leave a legacy by what we invest in others. Ministering, serving, supporting, encouraging. These are the actions and attitudes that will outlive us long after we're gone. We'll learn how to best help others struggling to deal with their own trials.

Discuss the Weekly Topics

Week Two: When I'm Doubted

You can't go through life many years without someone doubting you. Others made wrong assumptions about Job, too. Naysayers questioned him. They didn't offer the benefit of the doubt, which I like to call *the benefit of grace*. What can we learn from Job and other Bible passages that will help us when our own conflicts surface? How can we overcome feeling hurt and avoid growing bitter? How will this experience help us prevent future misunderstandings from occurring?

Week Three: When I'm Disrespected

Job's so-called friends judged and condemned him for sins he never committed. How can Scripture help us as we endure false allegations and grown-up bullying? Is there something we can learn to prevent it? How can we reach out to our enemies and reach out to other victims too?

Week Four: When I'm Deserted

Job must have felt alone. He lost all his family except his wife, and she wanted him to curse God and die. His friends let him down. A religious leader was no help. If you've ever felt invisible or abandoned, this chapter is for you. Sadly, we don't outgrow cliquish behavior—most adults face a time when they don't feel accepted. What does God want us to learn from these times, and how can we help others who endure isolation, so they don't feel alone?

Week Five: When I'm Deceived

Job received advice from five individuals. As accurate as their words sounded, they weren't appropriate for the setting. Today, more and more believers are attacked by spiritual abuse from ministers, church leaders, or other false teachers. In this chapter you'll be encouraged to discern truth and learn to reject spiritual advice that is twisted or distorted. And you'll receive soothing comfort as you seek to heal from the spiritual bullies of your past, so you can help others who are going through the same nightmare.

Week Six: When I'm Disappointed

While there's not much mention of it in Job, we can see that he was frustrated by his remaining relationships after his children all died on the same day. It's safe to say he dealt with unmet and unrealistic expectations with his wife and friends. In this chapter we'll address the hurts that hit closest to home—those inflicted on us by, or because of, the ones we love most. We'll deal with these disappointments, learn to adjust our expectations of others, and help them adjust their expectations of us.

Week Seven: When I'm Disabled

Not only did Job lose his relationships, he lost his health. He suffered excruciating symptoms, and when he needed the comfort of others the most, they ostracized him. Anyone who deals with acute or chronic health conditions can relate. Learn new coping skills as you suffer, and allow yourself to grieve the loss of your health. Then, with a healthy perspective, reach out to others who are enduring similar afflictions.

Week Eight: When I'm Destitute

Satan wiped out all of Job's possessions and material goods. He had to start from scratch. If you've ever lost a job, a home, or had a financial reversal, you know the challenge of starting over. What words of comfort and strength can you find from Scripture to help you hold on to hope? This chapter will help you when you feel destitute and equip you to encourage others as they face similar challenges.

Family Hope Chest

At the end of the book there is a section called *Family Hope Chest* that includes resources to help you as you deal with trials.

Focus Verse:

Don't forget our main Scripture concept as we study the types of trials Job faced. *No test or temptation that comes your way is beyond the course of what others have had to face. All you need to remember is that God will never let you down; he'll never let you be pushed past your limit; he'll always be there to help you come through it* (1 Corinthians 10:13 MSG).

Grin Gal Pal Time

Draw names to pair up into Grin Gal Pals. You can keep the same Grin Gal Pal for the entire study or draw new pairs each week. Encourage and pray for your pal. See each other as accountability partners for any of the action steps you decide to take in *Guide to Trials.* The more transparent you are during your Grin Gal time, the more support you'll receive as you face up to the trials going on in your everyday lives.

After group time, attendees will meet in pairs and discuss these points:

- One prayer request for the coming week.

- One thought that surfaced from your study time (either a concept, a challenge, or another way God is at work).

- One action step for dealing with personal trials better.

Ask Grin Gal Pals to connect for prayer and encouragement with each other during this study. This can be done through text, voice message, email, lunch date or greeting card note. The method can be as varied as the group—it doesn't have to be the same for everyone.

Assignment

Read Chapter One before the group's next meeting. Answer the questions to enhance your individual study and to prepare for group discussion time.

Closing Prayer

Heavenly Father, we ask that you help each lady here feel comfortable opening up about her trials, so she can receive the support she needs to cope and hope. As she reads through the first chapter this week, reveal to her the truths you want her to see, and encourage her heart. As we prepare to gather next time, help us not get distracted or discouraged and miss the discussion. Bring us together, so we can be there for each other. May no one feel like they are going it alone. Thank you for providing the peace and comfort we need to overcome what is overwhelming us. Amen.

WEEK TWO: WHEN I'M DOUBTED

Mixer

- What story stands out to you the most from this week's readings? Why?

- What Bible verse gave you an aha moment? Share the Bible verse and your insight.

- What principle from this chapter do you want to implement more in your own life?

Discussion Questions

- Which is more supportive, for a friend to sit by you in silence or for a friend to offer you their perspective on why you are suffering? What if their advice is based on distorted perceptions? What if you didn't ask for advice—in fact, you didn't ask for them to come?

- Can you think of a time when you felt misunderstood? How did it make you feel? How did you handle it?

- What are some ways you can communicate to others when they misunderstand you?

- Have you ever assumed the wrong thing about someone going through a tough time? Describe the situation and the outcome.

- Are you a fixer? Do you tend to offer advice rather than offering true support? What has this discussion revealed to you about that?

- How can you help others who are feeling doubted?

Focus Verse:

Don't forget our main Scripture concept as we study the types of trials Job faced. *No test or temptation that comes your way is beyond the course of what others have had to face. All you need to remember is that God will never let you down; he'll never let you be pushed past your limit; he'll always be there to help you come through it* (1 Corinthians 10:13 MSG).

Grin Gal Pal Time

Draw names to pair up into Grin Gal Pals. You can keep the same Grin Gal Pal for the entire study or draw new pairs each week. Encourage and pray for your pal. See each other as accountability partners for any of the action steps you decide to take in *Guide to Trials*. The more transparent you are during your Grin Gal time, the more support you'll receive as you face up to the trials going on in your everyday lives.

After group time, attendees will meet in pairs and discuss these points:

- One prayer request for the coming week.

- One thought that surfaced from your study time (either a concept, a challenge, or another way God is at work).

- One action step for dealing with personal trials better.

Ask Grin Gal Pals to connect for prayer and encouragement with each other during this study. This can be done through text, voice message, email, lunch date or greeting card note. The method can be as varied as the group—it doesn't have to be the same for everyone.

Assignment

Read Chapter Two before the group's next meeting. Answer the questions to enhance your individual study and to prepare for group discussion time.

Closing Prayer

Father in heaven, so many of us related to this chapter's topic, because we have experienced the pain of being misunderstood and doubted. Yet we also know there are times we've been guilty of these same attitudes with others. Help us grow as we seek your principles for dealing with this.

We have a hope that is anchored in *you*, not in our own strengths or abilities. May we put down our human tendencies, pick up your godliness, and put on your lovingkindness, so we can adopt your attitudes and actions.

And Father—so many of us are exhausted in our obedience rather than energized in our efforts to please you and deal with all this life stuff. Help us make sure we are doing this in your strength, so we don't run out of steam on the journey. Amen.

WEEK THREE: WHEN I'M DISRESPECTED

Mixer

- What story stands out to you the most from this week's readings? Why?

- What Bible verse gave you an aha moment? Share the Bible verse and your insight.

- What principle from this chapter do you want to implement more in your own life?

Discussion Questions

- If Job's friends were right (which they weren't), do you think they went about admonishing Job in the proper spirit? How should they have approached Job, if he *did* need to be aware of a shortcoming in his life?

- When you are faltering, how do you hope another will come alongside you to help pull you up out of your situation?

- When you feel impressed to help another brother or sister with their spiritual defeats and flaws, how do you think it's best to approach them?

- Think of the last time you caught yourself being judgmental. What motivated your attitude? How did you handle your thoughts? How did the way you managed your attitude lead to specific actions (for the good or for the bad)?

- What do you think happens when you address your own flaws before you start to deal with the ones others are guilty of?

- How can you help others who are feeling disrespected?

Focus Verse:

Don't forget our main Scripture concept as we study the types of trials Job faced. *No test or temptation that comes your way is beyond the course of what others have had to face. All you need to remember is that God will never let you down; he'll never let you be pushed past your limit; he'll always be there to help you come through it* (1 Corinthians 10:13 MSG).

Grin Gal Pal Time

Draw names to pair up into Grin Gal Pals. You can keep the same Grin Gal Pal for the entire study or draw new pairs each week. Encourage and pray for your pal. See each other as accountability partners for any of the action steps you decide to take in *Guide to Trials*. The more transparent you are during your Grin Gal time, the more support you'll receive as you face up to the trials going on in your everyday lives.

After group time, attendees will meet in pairs and discuss these points:

- One prayer request for the coming week.

- One thought that surfaced from your study time (either a concept, a challenge, or another way God is at work).

- One action step for dealing with personal trials better.

Ask Grin Gal Pals to connect for prayer and encouragement with each other during this study. This can be done through text, voice message, email, lunch date or greeting card note. The method can be as varied as the group—it doesn't have to be the same for everyone.

Assignment

Read Chapter Three before the group's next meeting. Answer the questions to enhance your individual study and to prepare for group discussion time.

Closing Prayer

Father, I have no words today other than "Help!" My heart grieves over the pain being suffered by members of our group. Bless all of us in a way that's unpredictable. Surprise us with your goodness in such a bold way that none of us can miss it in our lives. Help us cling to you when we fail everything else and we have no other support. Help us get to the point where we realize you really are *enough* for what we perceive as our *lack*. Amen.

WEEK FOUR: WHEN I'M DESERTED

Mixer

- What story stands out to you the most from this week's readings? Why?

- What Bible verse gave you an aha moment? Share the Bible verse and your insight.

- What principle from this chapter do you want to implement more in your own life?

Discussion Questions

- List five ways you relate to Psalm 22, and five ways this passage inspires you when you are feeling alone. Do you see a prayer to pray, an action to take, or a thought to focus on?

- What might God want you to learn about your moments of loneliness—those times when you feel all alone in this world, whether you're by yourself or in a crowd of people?

- Are you guilty of brushing off people because of your busy schedule or because you have your guard up to avoid being hurt again? How can you avoid making other people feel cut off from you?

- How can you help others who are feeling deserted?

Focus Verse:

Don't forget our main Scripture concept as we study the types of trials Job faced. *No test or temptation that comes your way is beyond the course of what others have had to face. All you need to remember is that God will never let you down; he'll never let you be pushed past your limit; he'll always be there to help you come through it* (1 Corinthians 10:13 MSG).

Grin Gal Pal Time

Draw names to pair up into Grin Gal Pals. You can keep the same Grin Gal Pal for the entire study or draw new pairs each week. Encourage and pray for your pal. See each other as accountability partners for any of the action steps you decide to take in *Guide to Trials*. The more transparent you are during your Grin Gal time, the more support you'll receive as you face up to the trials going on in your everyday lives.

After group time, attendees will meet in pairs and discuss these points:

- One prayer request for the coming week.

- One thought that surfaced from your study time (either a concept, a challenge, or another way God is at work).

- One action step for dealing with personal trials better.

Ask Grin Gal Pals to connect for prayer and encouragement with each other during this study. This can be done through text, voice message, email, lunch date or greeting card note. The method can be as varied as the group—it doesn't have to be the same for everyone.

Assignment

Read Chapter Four before the group's next meeting. Answer the questions to enhance your individual study and to prepare for group discussion time.

Closing Prayer

Father in heaven, we come to you today and ask that you take care of us. Be with us as we face our burdens head-on with the new perspectives you give us. Help us acknowledge the very things we'd like to forget about in our lives, whether they happened today or many years ago. Show us how to hang on when our circumstances separate us from the comfort of feeling loved by you and others. Remove the "invisi-shield" so we can be seen—not for our own glory or pride—but so we can be a part of your effective kingdom work. Be the *balm in Gilead* that soothes our wounds and dries our tears. Help us be aware of the others feeling like outcasts around us—that we might reach out to them and show them they can belong to you. Thank you that we are never alone—even when it feels as if we are. Amen.

WEEK FIVE: WHEN I'M DECEIVED

Mixer

- What story stands out to you the most from this week's readings? Why?

- What Bible verse gave you an aha moment? Share the Bible verse and your insight.

- What principle from this chapter do you want to implement more in your own life?

Discussion Questions

Note: When I ask about your involvement with a spiritual leader in the following questions, I mean it in the broadest sense. It could be a spouse who uses religious teachings for control, pastors, deacons, or other church members—any time a powerful person uses twisted teachings on God and Scripture to manipulate you or someone you know. Others in this definition include employers, supervisors, and those in Christian media (authors, television personalities, and those who have radio programs). Anyone who has the opportunity to mislead you.

- Have you been previously wounded by a spiritual leader? How long did it take to wise up to the error of their ways? What was your biggest struggle with it?

- Are you currently going through a trial caused by a spiritual leader? What is your biggest struggle with it?

- What advice would you tell a friend who's going through a situation like that today?

- How can we guard our own views of Scripture and God to make sure we do not use it to deceive others?

- How can you help others who are feeling deceived?

Focus Verse:

Don't forget our main Scripture concept as we study the types of trials Job faced. *No test or temptation that comes your way is beyond the course of what others have had to face. All you need to remember is that God will never let you down; he'll never let you be pushed past your limit; he'll always be there to help you come through it* (1 Corinthians 10:13 MSG).

Grin Gal Pal Time

Draw names to pair up into Grin Gal Pals. You can keep the same Grin Gal Pal for the entire study or draw new pairs each week. Encourage and pray for your pal. See each other as accountability partners for any of the action steps you decide to take in *Guide to Trials*. The more transparent you are during your Grin Gal time, the more support you'll receive as you face up to the trials going on in your everyday lives.

After group time, attendees will meet in pairs and discuss these points:

- One prayer request for the coming week.

- One thought that surfaced from your study time (either a concept, a challenge, or another way God is at work).

- One action step for dealing with personal trials better.

Ask Grin Gal Pals to connect for prayer and encouragement with each other during this study. This can be done through text, voice message, email, lunch date or greeting card note. The method can be as varied as the group—it doesn't have to be the same for everyone.

Assignment

Read Chapter Five before the group's next meeting. Answer the questions to enhance your individual study and to prepare for group discussion time.

Closing Prayer

Our Father who leads with grace, help us to have discernment with any leaders using Scripture with authority. Show us what we need to see. Direct us if you want us to get out of the situation or if you want us to speak up. Also, help us as we lead others, so that we do not manipulate biblical principles to fit a personal agenda. Comfort hearts and heal wounds as only you can. Amen.

WEEK SIX: WHEN I'M DISAPPOINTED

Mixer

- What story stands out to you the most from this week's readings? Why?

- What Bible verse gave you an aha moment? Share the Bible verse and your insight.

- What principle from this chapter do you want to implement more in your own life?

Discussion Questions

- According to Philippians 4:6–7, what are you to add to our prayers to prevent worry (anxiety)? What do you need to tell God? What will he do for you when you've done all this?

- How might you adjust your expectations in others, so you aren't hurt as often when they don't measure up to your hopes for them?

- Other than communication flaws, what other elements cause expectations to be more trying than usual?

- Are you experiencing a toxic relationship? What can you do about it?

- How do you handle stressful relationship situations when you have no control over the outcome?

- How can you help others who are dealing with disappointment?

Focus Verse:

Don't forget our main Scripture concept as we study the types of trials Job faced. *No test or temptation that comes your way is beyond the course of what others have had to face. All you need to remember is that God will never let you down; he'll never let you be pushed past your limit; he'll always be there to help you come through it* (1 Corinthians 10:13 MSG).

Grin Gal Pal Time

Draw names to pair up into Grin Gal Pals. You can keep the same Grin Gal Pal for the entire study or draw new pairs each week. Encourage and pray for your pal. See each other as accountability partners for any of the action steps you decide to take in *Guide to Trials*. The more transparent you are during your Grin Gal time, the more support you'll receive as you face up to the trials going on in your everyday lives.

After group time, attendees will meet in pairs and discuss these points:

- One prayer request for the coming week.

- One thought that surfaced from your study time (either a concept, a challenge, or another way God is at work).

- One action step for dealing with personal trials better.

Ask Grin Gal Pals to connect for prayer and encouragement with each other during this study. This can be done through text, voice message, email, lunch date or greeting card note. The method can be as varied as the group—it doesn't have to be the same for everyone.

Assignment

Read Chapter Six before the group's next meeting. Answer the questions to enhance your individual study and to prepare for group discussion time.

Closing Prayer

Father, we often have more questions than answers. More hurts than remedies. In our honesty, we bring to you the frustrations of our hearts. We're overwhelmed. Stressed. Yes, even licking our wounds at times rather than letting them go. We can't do life on our own. Equip us with what we need to survive these relationship disappointments. Sometimes we can walk away from unhealthy friendships, and sometimes we're related to the ones who make us feel so neglected or agitated. Tear down our walls—the walls we build to hide from you—and the walls we put up to avoid others. We even barricade our own hearts and minds to try to dull the pain. Knock them all down. Show us the relationships in which you want us to invest our time and emotion. Let it begin with our time and honest dialogue with you. Amen.

WEEK SEVEN: WHEN I'M DISABLED

Mixer

- What story stands out to you the most from this week's readings? Why?

- What Bible verse gave you an aha moment? Share the Bible verse and your insight.

- What principle from this chapter do you want to implement more in your own life?

Discussion Questions

- Read the testimony of Asaph in Psalm 73:1–28.

- Asaph was upset about a certain unfairness in life. What was it?

- Read verses 1–15. What verse do you most relate to when you are in a "woe is me" mood?

- Read verses 16–20, 27. What eventually happens to those who aren't part of God's family? Do they continue to prosper and not face suffering?

- Read verses 21–28. Like Asaph, list your shortcomings. Next, find all the reasons you can praise God even when you are suffering, based on this passage.

- The passage ends with a promise to tell others of God's goodness. How can you, in the midst of your suffering, find the right words (and mean them) to tell others about the wonderful works of God?

- How can you help others who are disabled with chronic symptoms?

Focus Verse:

Don't forget our main Scripture concept as we study the types of trials Job faced. *No test or temptation that comes your way is beyond the course of what others have had to face. All you need to remember is that God will never let you down; he'll never let you be pushed past your limit; he'll always be there to help you come through it* (1 Corinthians 10:13 MSG).

Grin Gal Pal Time

Draw names to pair up into Grin Gal Pals. You can keep the same Grin Gal Pal for the entire study or draw new pairs each week. Encourage and pray for your pal. See each other as accountability partners for any of the action steps you decide to take in *Guide to Trials*. The more transparent you are during your Grin Gal time, the more support you'll receive as you face up to the trials going on in your everyday lives.

After group time, attendees will meet in pairs and discuss these points:

- One prayer request for the coming week.

- One thought that surfaced from your study time (either a concept, a challenge, or another way God is at work).

- One action step for dealing with personal trials better.

Ask Grin Gal Pals to connect for prayer and encouragement with each other during this study. This can be done through text, voice message, email, lunch date or greeting card note. The method can be as varied as the group—it doesn't have to be the same for everyone.

Assignment

Read Chapter Seven and conclusion before the group's next meeting. Answer the questions to enhance your individual study and to prepare for group discussion time.

Closing Prayer

Father, we bring you all the physical suffering our group experiences. All the pain and symptoms our loved ones deal with on a regular basis. Chronic anything is just plain awful! We yield it to you for you to bring glory to yourself and to expand your kingdom. Help us not wallow in our trials and symptoms but find a way to rejoice that we join Jesus in the fellowship of his suffering. And help us be alert to the opportunities you give us, so we shine the light on you when others are hurting. Amen.

WEEK EIGHT: WHEN I'M DESTITUTE

Mixer

- What story stands out to you the most from this week's readings? Why?

- What Bible verse gave you an aha moment? Share the Bible verse and your insight.

- What principle from this chapter do you want to implement more in your own life?

Discussion Questions

- Can you think of a belonging that was damaged or lost that caused your heart to hurt? Why did it bother you so much? How did you get past it?

- Is it wrong to enjoy the blessings of material possessions? At what point is a love of "things" inappropriate for Christ followers?

- Have you ever found your reactions about belongings to be out of balance? How did you readjust?

- If you had to start over because of a financial reversal or loss of home or job—how did it go? If you could do anything over, what would you do differently?

- How can you help others who are destitute with loss of a job, possessions, or a home?

Focus Verse:

Don't forget our main Scripture concept as we study the types of trials Job faced. *No test or temptation that comes your way is beyond the course of what others have had to face. All you need to remember is that God will never let you down; he'll never let you be pushed past your limit; he'll always be there to help you come through it* (1 Corinthians 10:13 MSG).

Grin Gal Pal Time

Draw names to pair up into Grin Gal Pals. You can keep the same Grin Gal Pal for the entire study or draw new pairs each week. Encourage and pray for your pal. See each other as accountability partners for any of the action steps you decide to take in *Guide to Trials*. The more transparent you are during your Grin Gal time, the more support you'll receive as you face up to the trials going on in your everyday lives.

After group time, attendees will meet in pairs and discuss these points:

- One prayer request for the coming week.

- One thought that surfaced from your study time (either a concept, a challenge, or another way God is at work).

- One action step for dealing with personal trials better.

Final Prayer

Lord of my heart, I seek you on behalf of this group of gals, to help each of us in the way we deal with trials and how we help others going through trials. Most of all, help us not lose sight of you when a trial tries to cloud our view of you. I pray for each grin gal in the group—that you will comfort them and strengthen them when it comes to the trials they are facing right now. Equip them for what is ahead, and use them in such amazing ways we can only point to you as the Orchestrator of our days. Amen.

Wrap-Up Party

Decide how you want to close out this study. Invite me to join you via Zoom, Skype, or FaceTime if you want the attendees to have a chance to discuss the book with me. Or adopt a project to help a family or community going through a significant trial. Have a party (in real life or a virtual celebration). Give closure to this meaningful time the grin gals have had together.

ACKNOWLEDGEMENTS

This is the part of the book I always enjoy getting to— acknowledging the ones who contributed to the completion of this project. I'm sending grateful gratitudes to the following people and places:

Family. We have lived through many trials but also made wonderful memories. Everyday happenings and special events all contributed to my growing-up years of childhood and the sometimes groaning-up years of adulthood. You helped to shape me into the woman I am today.

My focus group. You were the first to read the book and joined me in asking, "Is Job a member of my family tree?" Thank you for testing it and offering feedback. Because of your transparency, you made the book better. Gratitude goes out to: Robin Steinweg, Deanna Smith, Hally Wells, Vickie Price Taylor, Kim Whaley, Sandra Reid Bassett, Robin Grunder, and Luanne Lopez.

My faith family at Praise Church, especially my **Faith & Friends Book Club**. You helped nudge this book into existence with your prayers and support.

My wisdom team. You support me with your notes, calls, prayers, and wise words. Special acknowledgement goes to Jessica Caudill, Sally Ferguson, Stephenie Hovland, Michelle Rayburn, Laurie Ritchel, Robin Steinweg, and Gina Stinson.

Joy Weese Moll, my writing buddy. Thanks for giving me the accountability I needed to stay focused on finishing this book.

My pull-quote team. You mined the gold nuggets from this book to help me choose the book's pull quotes and the meme quotes for later on. And just when I needed it, you gave me an atta-girl. Your belief that this book would make a difference in others made a difference in me. Thanks to Tracy Parmenter, Lori Garza, Jennifer Romero, Jessica Caudill, Laurie Ritchel, Stephenie Hovland, Robin Steinweg, and Sally Ferguson.

My editor, Stephenie Hovland. Thanks for polishing my words and making them shine. This book is better because of you.

My book designer, Michelle Rayburn. Thank you for designing the Grin Gal brand and creating a winsome look to my covers and interior design. You really get me!

My husband, Russ. We've lived through so many trials together and I still want to do life with you every single day. Thanks for being by my side all the way.

Jesus Christ my Savior and Lord. Thank you for helping my heart grin despite the challenges. You are the reason I look forward to every day. May *7 Trials Every Woman Faces* glorify you.

ABOUT THE AUTHOR

God's Grin Gal, Kathy Carlton Willis, writes and speaks with a balance of funny and faith, whimsy and wisdom. She coaches others to remove the training wheels of fear and not just risk, but also take pleasure in the joy ride of life. She is known for her debut book, *Grin with Grace* and for her grinning Boston Terrier, Hettie.

Not many funny girls also have Bible degrees! She graduated with honors from Bible College, holding degrees in Bible and Church Education, and served for thirty years in full-time church ministry with her pastor/husband, Russ. She's active as a book industry pro, while also staying involved in her church.

Kathy works with women's groups and writers' groups, inside and outside the church. She's passionate about helping believers have "aha! moments" with the daily application of Scripture.

Even with all the circumstances she's faced, she gives a very clear message that she possesses an expectant hope and contentment in the Lord. Something we can all experience.

Kathy Carlton Willis owns KCW Communications, spinning many plates as writer, editor, speaker, and coach. Over 1,000 of her writing projects have appeared online and in print publications.

CBN.com features Kathy's popular blog. Their website consistently ranks among the top 10 most popular sites in the Lifestyle— Religion category. *Grin & Grow with Kathy* offers a twice-monthly devo-study utilizing her story, study, and steps format.

She is a contributing writer for *Upgrade Your Life*, *The Christian Communicator*, *The Christian Pulse*, along with others. Kathy also writes inspirational, motivational and transparent posts and videos on social media.

Kathy founded WordGirls, a community of Christian female writers who receive professional coaching from Kathy.

She writes and speaks on the issues that hold believers back and shines the light on their path to freedom. Kathy shines, whether she's shining the light on God's writers and speakers, or reflecting God's light during her speaking opportunities.

Learn more at Kathy's website: kathycarltonwillis.com

3G BOOKS

In addition to *7 Trials Every Woman Faces,* Kathy Carlton Willis has started a line of books designed to release twice a year. Kathy's boldly practical tips, tools, and takeaways show up in Christian living books, Bible studies, and devo-studies. 3G Books are perfect for small groups or individual reading.

Earlier this year, 3G Books published *The Grin Gal's Guide to Joy.*

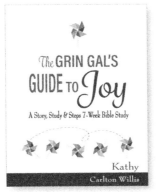

If you've ever felt like the joy, joy, joy, joy down in your heart has gone missing, then this book is for you!

Kathy learned that happiness runs and hides, but joy remains when trials show up. Now she's here to share these principles with you in *The Grin Gal's Guide to Joy.*

In each chapter:

- **Grin with Joy** tells real-life stories and observations. You'll laugh at Kathy's humorous confessions and wacky insights.

- **Grow with Joy** features a joy word study and workbook. Kathy explores what the Bible says and unpacks timely truths.

- **Go with Joy** offers life application. Pick the action steps that help you live a joy-filled life.

- **Give with Joy** equips you to share joy and meet the needs of others. This is when faith becomes ministry.

- **Your Grin with Joy Challenge** describes a joy-challenging scenario to solve.

Praise for the book:

"With her trademark honesty, warmth, wit, and humor, Kathy inspires us to grin with joy, regardless of our circumstances."

— **Christin Ditchfield,** radio host, speaker, and author of over 80 books

"Kathy Carlton Willis writes stories from her open-book life in a way that makes me want to say, 'She gets me! She really really *gets* me!'"

— **Pat Layton,** author, *Life Unstuck*

"With relatable stories of finding joy even in the challenges of life, Kathy leads the way with wonderful humor and refreshing honesty. Her joy is infectious!"

— **Julie Zine Coleman,** speaker, author and managing editor

"Kathy is humorously serious about joy! She doesn't just tell us why we can grin with joy; she shows us how to go out and live joyfully."

— **Kathy Howard,** speaker, Bible teacher and author

Buy *The Grin Gal's Guide to Joy* at **kathycarltonwillis.com**

The Ultimate Speaker's Guide

The first book to kick off 3G Books was created with speakers in mind. Packed cover-to-cover with invaluable information, *The Ultimate Speaker's Guide* is the new bible for communicators. With almost two decades of industry knowledge under her belt, Kathy Carlton Willis has coached hundreds of speakers to help them develop successful speaking businesses. This book covers all the tips, tools, and takeaways you'll need to ensure that your audience increases and your message is heard, including:

- Setting up your business
- Finding a brand that fits
- Getting more bookings
- Polishing your style
- Discovering God's plan for your business

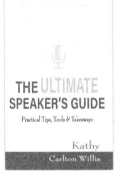

An extensive resource section containing a sample contract, media interviewing tips, fee schedules, checklists, and much more, makes *The Ultimate Speaker's Guide* an essential toolkit you'll use time and again.

Praise for the book:

"Whether you're new to speaking to promote the message God has given you or have been doing it for a while, you'll find a wealth of practical help in *The Ultimate Speaker's Guide*. Kathy's experience as a speaker and trainer fills a void in resources for Christian speakers."

> **– Lin Johnson,** Write-to-Publish Conference Director
> Managing Editor of *Christian Communicator*

Buy *The Ultimate Speaker's Guide* at **kathycarltonwillis.com**

Made in the USA
Monee, IL
18 August 2021